PLAY TOGETHER

LEARN TOGETHER

KINGFISHER
An imprint of Larousse plc
New Penderel House
283-288 High Holborn
London WC1V 7HZ

First published in 1985 by Kingfisher Books Ltd
This edition published 1998
Text © Melanie Rice 1985
Illustrations © Larousse 1985

A CIP catalogue record for this book is available from the British Library

ISBN 0 86272 119 9

Colour separations by Newsele Litho Ltd, Milan, Italy
Printed in Italy by Eurolitho

Editor: Jacqui Bailey
Assistant Editor: Deri Warren
Design: The Pinpoint Design Company
Photography: Rex Caves

Acknowledgements:
The author would like to thank her husband, Chris, for all his invaluable advice and support during
the preparation of this book.
The publishers would like to thank the staff and pupils of Hadrian Lower School, Dunstable, for their
help with some of the projects in the book.
For permission to include copyright material, acknowledgement and thanks for their help and
courtesy are due to the following:
Evelyn Abraham and A & C Black Publishers Ltd for 'Upstairs, Downstairs' from *Rhythm Rhymes*
Aileen Fisher and Abelard Press for 'Bird Talk' from *Up the Windy Hill,* New York 1953,
© renewed 1981
Daphne Lister and Corgi Books for 'In the Rain' from *Gingerbread Pigs and Other Rhymes,* © 1980
Spike Milligan and Spike Milligan Productions Ltd for 'Rain' and 'Bump' from *Silly Verse for Kids*
A A Milne and Methuen Children's Books for 'Lines and Squares' from *When We Were Very Young*
Ogden Nash and Curtis Brown Ltd for 'Hands' from *Family Reunion,* © Ogden Nash. Reproduced
on behalf of the estate of Ogden Nash by Curtis Brown Ltd, London
Laura E Richards and A & C Black Publishers Ltd for 'Eletelephony' from *Speech Rhymes*
Clive Sansom and A & C Black Publishers Ltd for 'The Airman', 'I Wish I Could',
'Rat-a-Tat-Tat' and 'Tea-time for Timothy' from *Speech Rhymes* and 'Walking' from *Rhythm Rhymes*
Ruth Sansom and A & C Black Publishers Ltd for 'Elephant Walk', 'Going to the Sea'
and 'Tippy Tippy' from *Rhythm Rhymes*
Ian Serraillier and Oxford University Press for 'The Tickle Rhyme' from *The Monster Horse* © 1950
Ian Serraillier and Oxford University Press
Robert Louis Stevenson and Puffin Books for 'Bed in Summer' from *A Child's Garden of Verse*
While every effort has been made to obtain permission, there may still be cases in
which we have failed to trace a copyright holder, and we would like to apologise
for any apparent negligence.

PLAY TOGETHER LEARN TOGETHER

MELANIE RICE

Illustrated by **Chris Barker**
Adviser **Betty Root**

KING*f*ISHER

Contents

Art and craft ideas

Gathering materials   *page 10*
Painting   *page 12*
Magic painting   *page 14*
Finger painting   *page 15*
Making prints   *page 16*
Collage   *page 20*
Paper collage   *page 22*
Paper patterns   *page 24*
Models   *page 25*
Cut-out dolls   *page 26*
Toys and sculptures   *page 28*
Mobiles   *page 30*
Papier-mâché   *page 31*
Models   *page 32*
A play house   *page 34*
An obstacle course   *page 35*
A doll's house   *page 36*
Threading and tying   *page 38*
Weaving   *page 41*
Woodwork   *page 42*

Exploring further

Around the house   *page 44*
Cooking   *page 45*
Beginners' recipes   *page 46*
More about food   *page 49*
Know your body   *page 52*
Playing with water   *page 55*
Water games   *page 56*
Weighing   *page 57*
Out of doors   *page 58*
Things to collect   *page 60*
Learn about growing   *page 62*
Observing animals   *page 65*
Animal homes   *page 66*
Feeding signs   *page 67*
Looking at birds   *page 68*
Making a bird table   *page 69*
Keeping pets   *page 70*
Whatever the weather   *page 75*
Make a weather calendar
   page 79
The seasons   *page 80*
What to wear   *page 81*

Matching and making pairs

Colour   *page 84*
A colour game   *page 85*
Shapes   *page 86*
Sizes   *page 88*
Games to play   *page 90*
Goldilocks and the three
   bears   *page 91*
Things that go together
   page 92
Mix and muddle   *page 94*
Jigsaws   *page 96*
Making your own cards
   page 97
Card games   *page 99*

Numbers and counting

The meaning of numbers
   page 104
Number games   *page 107*
Board games   *page 108*
Making dice and spinners
   page 109
Number rhymes   *page 110*
Recognizing and writing
   numbers   *page 112*
Measuring   *page 114*
Telling the time   *page 115*
Today, tomorrow   *page 116*

Music and listening

earning to listen   *page 118*
hythm games   *page 119*
usic and movement   *age 120*
aking instruments   *page 123*
stening to music   *page 126*

Play-acting

Finger and hand puppets
   page 128
String and stick puppets
   page 131
Hinged and shadow puppets
   page 132
Making masks   *page 134*
Dressing up   *page 135*
Acting games   *page 136*

Word-building and story–telling

Using words   *page 140*
Action poems   *page 143*
Scrapbooks   *page 144*
Shaping letters   *page 145*
Making friezes   *page 146*
Animal shapes   *page 147*
Picture stories   *page 149*
Story ideas   *page 150*
Other ways to illustrate
   stories   *page 152*

Preparing to read and write

Getting started   *page 154*
Observing details   *page 156*
Learning letters   *page 157*
Letter games   *page 158*
Learning words   *page 159*
Word games   *page 160*

Preface

Most parents understand that *time* is the most important gift they can give to their children. Time spent on activities outside of the daily chores is rewarding for parents also, allowing the opportunity to observe and enjoy the different stages of their child's development. But parents are busy people, and it is not always easy to find the time, especially when faced with the question 'What can we do today?'.

Here, at last, is a book which really does help. 'Play Together, Learn Together' is a treasure chest of sparkling ideas, brimming with practical suggestions and clear instructions. It is obvious that the author has only included those ideas which have been thoroughly tried and tested, avoiding the kind of complicated projects which so often lead to disappointments.

This is not the kind of book which you need to work through page by page. The real fun is to dip into it when you feel like it, to do whatever appeals the most. You will find a wealth of ideas to help your child and to help you. Enjoy it together.

BETTY ROOT

About this book

'Play Together, Learn Together' is a compilation of ideas drawn from my experience of bringing up two young children. It was then that I discovered at first hand just how long the hours can seem between breakfast and bedtime! With household chores and demanding minds competing for my attention all day, I usually found that, despite good intentions, a backward glance showed how very little of my time was spent actually playing with the children. I hope that this book will provide parents who also have 'good intentions' with a source of reference; inspiring them to make the most of the rewarding hours spent in the company of their pre-school children.

Parent and Child Together
As the title suggests, play should always be to the mutual benefit of child and parent. Parents learn a great deal about their children by observing them while they play and by listening to them recalling their experiences. Listening is particularly important; while it is easy to talk to children, listening requires more patience – it's all too tempting to interrupt or finish sentences which seem to falter or stray from the point.

Children learn from their parents through conversation as well as through other stimuli – poems, pictures, games and so on. And because of the special intimacy which exists between parent and child, each activity can be directly related to the world they share.

But do remember that the emphasis in this book is on the word 'play'. Children learn much more quickly and easily when they are absorbed and interested in what they are doing. Never try to force your child into an activity; if they begin to get bored, do something else. Children are also quick to pick up on the moods of their parents, so if *you* are bored that is also a good reason to do something else. Try not to feel that you and your child ought to do these activities simply because they may be 'educational'.

Using This Book
In making the selection of activities for this book I have tried to include only those which are readily accessible, which generally need little preparation and which use materials close to hand, and which do not require special outings to provide stimulation.

The activities have not been arranged according to age; this type of categorization seemed irrelevent to me, as every child has a different rate of development. No doubt you too will have been irritated by being told that a 'three-year-old should be able to . . . . .' when it's clear that, whatever the activity, children proceed at their own pace. While no amount of pushing can force them to begin learning before they're ready, once they've started it is impossible to stop them.

I suggest that you use this book rather like a cookery book, mixing the activities from each section to provide a 'balanced diet'.

A Few Tips
Before starting a play session, bear the following in mind:
1. Atmosphere – a happy relaxed atmosphere is essential if a child is going to benefit from the session.
2. Timing – a tired or hungry child will

be inattentive, while interruptions spoil concentration.

3. Location – many activities need plenty of room; paints and other equipment, including things for mopping up, need to be on hand.

Once a child becomes engrossed in what they are doing the hardest moment arrives for the parent. A balance has to be struck between helping and interfering. It's not easy to sit back and watch children explore and discover, without succumbing to the temptation of imposing one's own ideas in order to speed up the process. Yet only by probing for themselves can children come to a real understanding of the world. It is very important that they are given the time to experiment; try to work alongside the child rather than lead.

Some Do's and Don'ts

Do encourage with constant praise.

Do display the best work where other members of the family can see and admire it.

Do be prepared to listen when your child wants to talk about their discoveries.

Do play only when they are interested.

Do introduce new ideas slowly and carefully.

Do give your child plenty of practice with any new skills.

Do restore their confidence when they fail to understand, by abandoning the activity (if possible, bringing it to a satisfactory conclusion), and then returning to something they know they can do well.

Don't try more than one new idea at a time; a subject can always be developed another day.

Don't take knowledge for granted.

Don't be impatient.

Don't linger over a game if your child becomes bored or if other distractions interfere (for example, children playing outside the window).

Don't use the games as a punishment . . . 'Now sit quietly and do this . . .'

What Will They Learn?

The ideas in this book have been designed to help children acquire a wide variety of skills, enabling them to explore and to interpret the world for themselves.

1. Speaking – vocabulary will increase with the desire to express new knowledge and with regular practice in communication. This in turn will bolster confidence in playgroup or school situations, where children constantly find themselves competing for attention.

2. Listening – the ability to follow simple instructions, to distinguish differences in sounds and to identify patterns of speech are all invaluable in language work.

3. Observing – when they begin to learn to read children need to be able to distinguish basic patterns and shapes, especially letter shapes (which are all written words mean to them). They also need to understand why the shapes are arranged in that way on the page, and the relationship of the shapes to one another.

4. Manual dexterity – the practised use of tools such as paintbrushes and pencils helps accustom children to the skill of writing and develops co-ordination.

Learning to Read

A dilemma faced by many parents is – should children be taught to read or write before they attend school? My own answer is simple, 'Yes, *if they want to'*. Here again, however, it is for each parent to recognize when their children are ready to take such a step. Some children are keen to learn early while others make no progress until they have settled in at school. It really doesn't matter if they can't read before starting school; what *is* important is that they develop an interest in and an affection for books. This can be fostered in several ways:

1. Set an example by reading yourself.

2. Cuddle up with your children and look at picture books – well-illustrated adult reference books as well as children's books.

3. Read stories to your children, encouraging them to work from left to right and pointing to the words as you read.

If your child seems ready to learn to read, then teach him or her yourself, but be careful to go slowly and gently, making the experience a pleasurable one.

Finally, whether you decide to try all the activities in this book, or just use a few of them as a basis for developing your own ideas, remember that the whole exercise can be, indeed ought to be, tremendous fun.

MELANIE RICE

Art and craft ideas

Gathering materials

Here are some ideas for building up your 'art box', but no doubt you will have plenty of others of your own.

As a general rule, introduce things to your child gradually—too much to choose from at any one time can be overwhelming. Occasionally put things away for a few months to prevent boredom.

To begin with, look around the house—even rubbish may turn out to be useful—so start collecting:

Containers
Lids from jars or aerosol cans, yoghurt pots, margarine or cottage cheese tubs, styrofoam meat trays, tin foil trays and other pre-packed food cartons, eggboxes, matchboxes, cupcake cases, tins—such as cocoa or plaster tins, with firm lids—and plastic bottles.

Paper
Newspaper, magazines, catalogues, old Christmas and birthday cards, postcards, tissue paper, foil, paper doilies, gift paper, computer print-out paper, wallpaper, cellophane, and straws.

Cardboard
Backs of notepads, corrugated card, toilet-roll cores, shirt card, cereal boxes.

Material Scraps
Any kind, but especially fur, tweed, lace, hessian, velvet, corduroy, old shirts or sheets, rug scraps, feathers, fringing, ribbons, sponge, wool.

Odds and Ends
String, shoelaces, rubber bands, pipe cleaners, buttons, beads, curtain rings, sequins, seeds, nuts, cereal, macaroni, cotton reels, iced-lolly sticks, toothpicks, woodshavings, corks, metal foil and plastic bottle tops.

Paint
1 Large plastic bottles of poster paint. Only put out a little to use at a time.

2 Powder paint. This is cheaper but messier. Mix it yourself to the thickness of double cream. If it dries out, add a few drops of hot water and leave for a couple of hours.

3 Water colour blocks. These come in boxes and are economical and clean to use. But they aren't good for experimentation with textures and are ineffective on top of coloured paper.

Painting Tips
When mixing paint it tends to go further if you add a few drops of cellulose wallpaper paste to it.

If you add a little detergent to paint it makes it easier to remove from clothes.

If you run out of paint, use flour mixed with water and food colouring.

Palettes for Holding Paint

Use yoghurt pots (or the tops of aerosol cans) placed on a tray. Or use an old baking tray with separate compartments.

Warning: When children first paint they splash their brush enthusiastically from one pot to the other until the paints become muddy. Don't interfere—they will soon realize that it's better to keep the colours separate.

Paste

1. Wallpaper paste. Cheap and useful for sticking paper together and for thickening paint.
2. Flour and water. Mix to a stodgy consistency.
3. PVA adhesive. Buy ready-mixed or in powder form. It sticks just about everything and washes out with water.

Brushes

1. Buy large sizes to encourage bold brush strokes.
2. Sometimes use 1 inch (about 2.5 cm) hardware brushes—they can be better than art brushes.
3. Keep a separate brush for paste, or use a piece of card.

Wash all brushes in soapy water when finished with, and store them flat in newspaper to keep their shape.

Crayons and Chalks

Buy extra-thick wax crayons and the thickest types of chalk and charcoal (they don't break so easily). Peel off any paper so that the sides can be used as well.

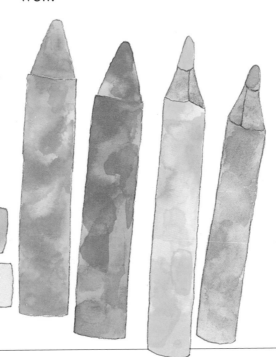

Clay or Dough

1. Clay of a type which hardens without being baked is now available, but it is very expensive.
2. Plasticine or 'Play Doh' is softer and easier to manipulate. You can make your own. At first, use the recipe that is given here, but later try experimenting with the amounts. It will keep indefinitely in an airtight plastic bag or pot.

Dough Recipe
2 cups flour
2 tbs cooking oil
1 cup water
1 cup salt
Add paint or food colouring as wanted.

Be Prepared

Before you start any kind of art activity, spread a large sheet of polythene across the floor. It can be bought quite cheaply by the metre from hardware shops and is well worth the money. Have a large bowl of soapy water, a sponge and a mop handy!

11

Painting

Think of different ways to apply the paint. Spatter and splash it on. Use your fingers (most children do naturally when they begin painting), or any of the following: a comb, a brush, a piece of card, a sponge, a toothbrush, string. Try putting some paint into the corner of a plastic bag. Cut a small hole in the bag and let the paint dribble onto the paper.

Experiment with interesting textures. Add soap powder, washing-up liquid, flour, sugar, sand, PVA adhesive or wallpaper paste to the paint and see what happens.

Vary the surface you paint on. Try foil, corrugated card, tissue paper, old magazines or newspaper, wet paper, paper brushed with cooking oil, or even cellophane—the finished product can then be hung on the window.

How to Teach Painting

The answer is, don't. It impedes natural creativity. The best you can do is to provide the materials and opportunities to stimulate the imagination and then take a back seat. Avoid asking questions like 'What is it?', or 'Tell me about it', when you are presented with a piece of paper apparently filled with meaningless splodges. When children paint they are expressing their feelings rather than representing particular objects; it is the act of painting that is important, rather than the finished product.

Blobbing Paint

Drop a few blobs of very thin paint onto a piece of paper and tilt it to form rivulets. As an alternative, blow paint over the paper with a straw.

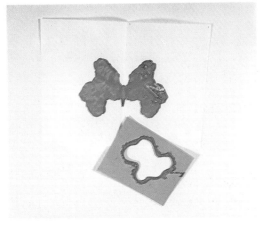

Bubbles

While you have a pot of thin paint to hand, mix some washing-up liquid into it and blow air into the pot through a small straw to make coloured bubbles on the surface. When you have a fairly frothy surface, gently lay a piece of paper over the top.

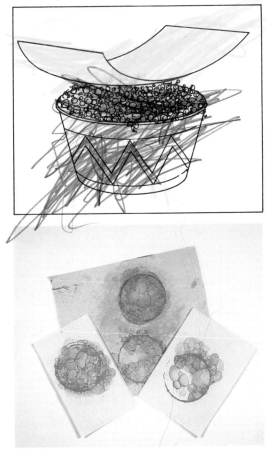

Stencils

A piece of sponge is ideal for applying paint to stencils.

1 Cut a random shape from the middle of a thick piece of card. Lay the card on a piece of paper and use it as a stencil by filling the hole with paint. Or, put the shape on the paper and paint around its edge.

Try folding the paper in half and smoothing your hand firmly over the top. On opening the paper, both sides will be identical.

2 For more intricate stencils use paper doilies. You can make your own by folding a circle of paper into quarters (as shown below) and cutting out a few simple shapes.

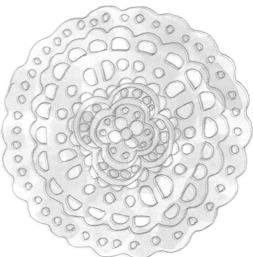

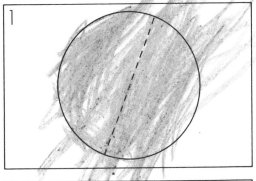

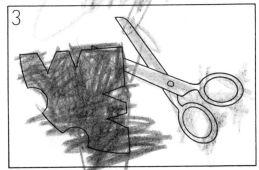

Magic painting

1 Place a thin piece of paper over any objects which have an interesting surface texture. Then rub firmly across the paper with the sides of a crayon until the pattern of the object appears.

3 Make a drawing with wax crayon, pressing heavily on the crayon. Wash over the paper with thin paint—the drawing will shine through.

For extra magic, follow the same procedure but this time use a white candle to make the drawing. The drawing will not show until the paint is applied.

2 With a spot of glue to stop them from slipping, stick some large magazine pictures onto a piece of card and cover with a sheet of white tissue paper. Paint water over the tissue, using a large brush, and watch the pictures appear.

4 Cover a sheet of strong paper or white card with brightly-coloured patches of wax crayon. Now completely cover the whole paper with black crayon. Scratch away the black to form patterns. You will need to use something with a fairly sharp point, such as a knitting needle.

Finger painting

Mix flour and powder paint with water to make a thick paint. Spread onto a sheet of firm paper, a smooth tray, or a baking tin, and let your child draw patterns in the paint with their fingers.

Colour Mixing
For older children. Put out two or three colours. Let your child decide which colours to use where. Talk about the different colour combinations he or she has made.

Making prints

First, you will need to make a paint pad. Mix some thick paint and add a pinch of wallpaper paste and a little detergent. Lay a piece of sponge or foam, or a piece of flannel in a tray (use a styrofoam meat tray or an old baking tray) and pour the paint over the sponge.

All kinds of objects will make prints. Press them firmly onto the paint pad and then onto the paper.

String Prints

1 Dip a piece of wool or string into the paint. Lay it on the paper with one end hanging over the edge. Fold the paper in half and, with one hand laid gently on top, slide out the piece of string.

2 Cover a cardboard tube with glue and wind a piece of string around the outside of the tube. When the glue is dry, roll the tube across the paint pad and then across a sheet of paper.

3 Dab PVA adhesive onto a piece of paper. Drop a few odd lengths of string onto the glued paper so that they fall into curled patterns. When the glue is dry, apply thick paint to the string. Take a print of the string pattern by placing another sheet of paper on top of the string and pressing down firmly with a rolling pin.

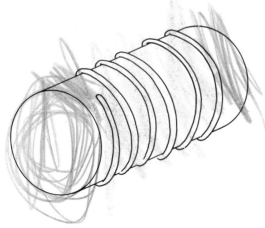

Hand and Foot Prints

Press feet and hands first onto the paint pad and then onto a large sheet of paper. Use fingerprints too, to make up a pattern.

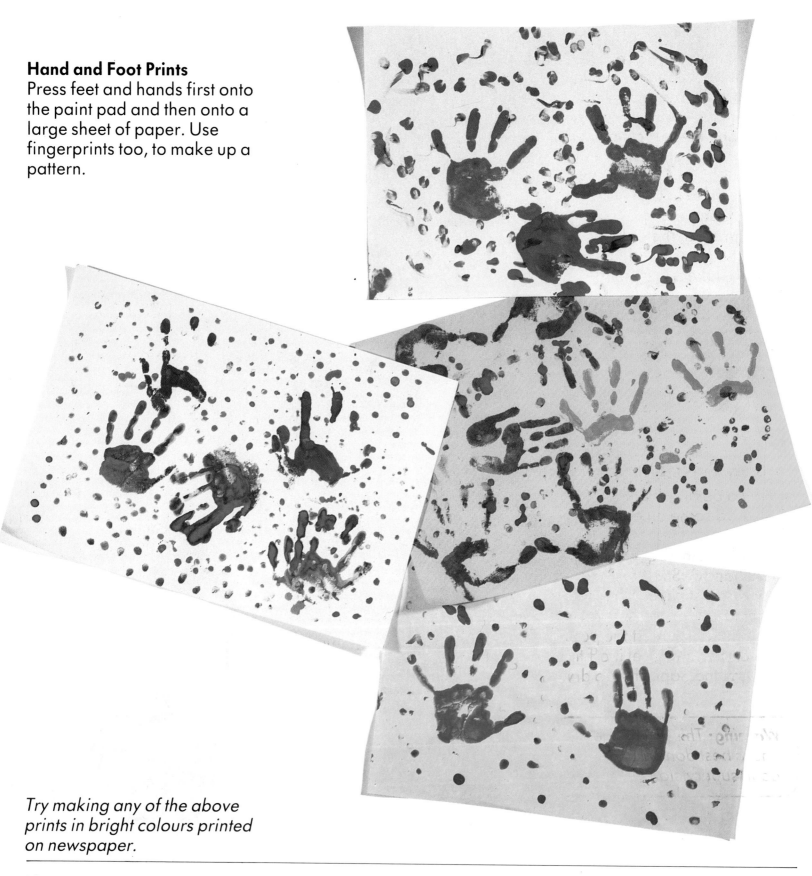

Try making any of the above prints in bright colours printed on newspaper.

Printing from Plastic

Spread a thick layer of paint mixed with PVA adhesive onto a piece of polythene. Scrape away patterns in the paint with a piece of card. Take a print by placing a sheet of paper over the polythene.

You can clean the polythene with washing-up liquid, but as you do so, take a print of the bubbles and swirls that form when you add the detergent.

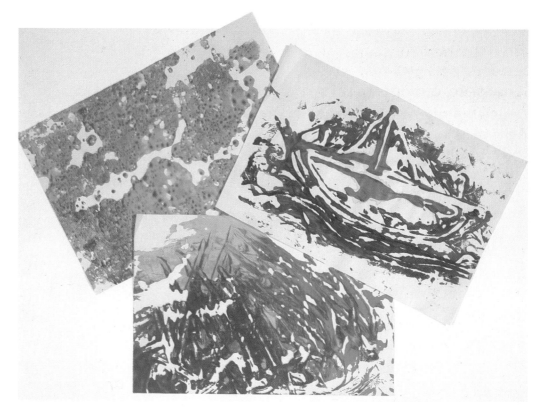

Oil on Water Prints

Half-fill a baking tray with water. Add some oil paints of different colours, or left-over household paint (but keep a solvent handy). Stir the water gently with a stick, and float a sheet of paper on the surface for half a minute. Then lift the paper at one corner and peel it off the water. Lay the paper flat to dry.

Warning: *This is very messy and is best done only with adult supervision.*

Collage

For young children, simply spread PVA adhesive over a piece of paper and place objects onto the surface.

Use buttons, wool, fabrics, pipe cleaners, feathers, bottle tops, seeds, dried peas, leaves, egg shells, etc.

Use different materials as a base: card, wood, or even a slab of dough, for example.

Older children can apply glue directly to the objects. Paint some objects before gluing them, or alternatively, paint over and round them onto the paper when the glue has dried.

String Collage
String, dipped into a thick mixture of paint and paste, will stick firmly as it dries.

Paper collage

A wide variety of shapes and textures can be obtained just from paper. Remember that it can be torn, cut, rolled, twisted, bent, folded, crumpled, fringed, pleated and curled.

Pleating
Lightly mark off a piece of paper into equal divisions. Fold along the marks.

Fringing
Alternatively, cut the paper three-quarters of the way along each division.

Spirals
Cut paper into a rough circle and mark out as shown. Cut along the marks and hang it vertically from the centre. Or, fasten at both ends so that it winds horizontally across the collage like a snake.

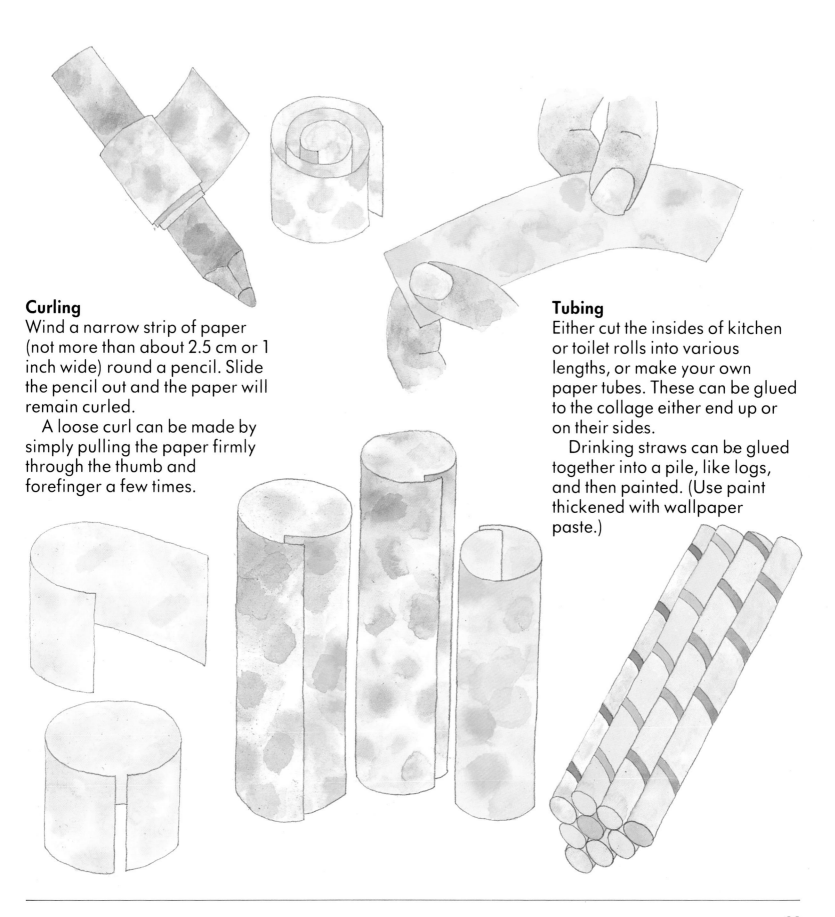

Curling

Wind a narrow strip of paper (not more than about 2.5 cm or 1 inch wide) round a pencil. Slide the pencil out and the paper will remain curled.

A loose curl can be made by simply pulling the paper firmly through the thumb and forefinger a few times.

Tubing

Either cut the insides of kitchen or toilet rolls into various lengths, or make your own paper tubes. These can be glued to the collage either end up or on their sides.

Drinking straws can be glued together into a pile, like logs, and then painted. (Use paint thickened with wallpaper paste.)

Paper patterns

Collect an assortment of paper, such as tissue paper, typing paper, silver foil, scrap paper, sugar paper, cardboard, cellophane and printed paper (newspapers, magazines, old letters, wrapping paper).

1 Make patterns using paper cut into one particular shape, such as all stars, or all circles.

2 Buy some clear plastic film which has a sticky 'peel-off' backing (you can get this from most art shops or good stationers). Tear up some pieces of tissue paper and apply them to the sticky side of the plastic. New colours can be made by overlapping two pieces of differently-coloured tissue. The final result can then be hung against a window so the light will shine through.

3 Cut silhouette shapes from black paper and stick them onto a coloured background. Or, you could colour in the background first with a finger painting.

Models

A young child can produce exciting sculptures and models using items from your art box; it does not matter at all if the early attempts are not recognizable.

Try making trains, cars, boats, people, monsters, etc. Allow your child's imagination to run riot—and before long, better models will appear than I could ever suggest.

Use cardboard boxes (for bases), tubes (for bodies or funnels), cotton reels and cheese boxes (heads or wheels), yoghurt pots (hats), pipe cleaners, string or drinking straws (arms and legs), plastic bottles (heads or bodies), and strips cut from washing-up-liquid bottles (arms or tentacles).

Cut-out dolls

Trace the picture of the doll shown here onto stiff card, and cut out around the dotted lines.

Either draw the clothes yourself for your child to colour in, or cut them from wallpaper samples—choose the patterns with your child.

Remember to cut the clothes with tags on each shoulder and on either side of the waist so they can be hung from the doll.

Toys and sculptures

Newspaper Trees
Roll up a sheet of newspaper and sellotape it lightly at one end to hold the roll in place. At the other end, use a pair of scissors to cut the roll into strips (from the centre out). Cut the strips about two-thirds down the length of the roll. Pull up the inside 'leaves', turning them slightly as you pull. The outside 'leaves' will spread out into the shape of a tree.

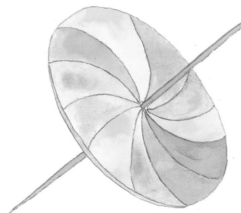

Whizzer Wheel
Cut out a circle of card (with a diameter of about 12 cm or 5 inches) and paint coloured shapes on it. Bore two holes in the centre and thread a piece of wool through them. Tie the wool so that the wheel is in the middle of two loops. Put each hand through a loop, and twist the wool as much as you can, holding one hand still while turning the other. Pull sharply so that the card spins round, then let it slacken. Continue jerking the wool and the wheel will spin.

Spinning Top
Cut out a circle of card and paint a pattern on it. An older child might try painting a spiral—you could draw the edges in first in pencil. Put a cocktail stick or pencil through the *centre* of the card and spin it.

Windmill
Paint or print bright patterns on both sides of a piece of thin card, about 15 cm or 6 inches square. Cut the paper from each corner to within about 2.5 cm or 1 inch of the centre, as shown.

Without creasing the paper, pull the left side of each corner into the centre. Thread a piece of fuse wire through all the layers of card at the centre, and twist the wire around a bead to secure the front.

Finally, thread a second bead onto the back and attach the wire firmly to the end of a stick.

Creeping Cotton Reels

Paint an empty cotton reel and put a thick rubber band through the hole. Place a short pencil inside each end of the band. Wind up one side, put the cotton reel on the table and watch it creep along.

Hole Sculptures

You will need some clay or plasticine to make a base, some tubes, and pieces of paper and card with holes cut in them.

Make some holes in the clay base with a pencil—make some of the holes go straight through the base. Push the cards, tubes and paper into the clay around the holes.

As an alternative, build up a sculpture using straws, toffee papers, chocolate-box wrappings and other see-through materials.

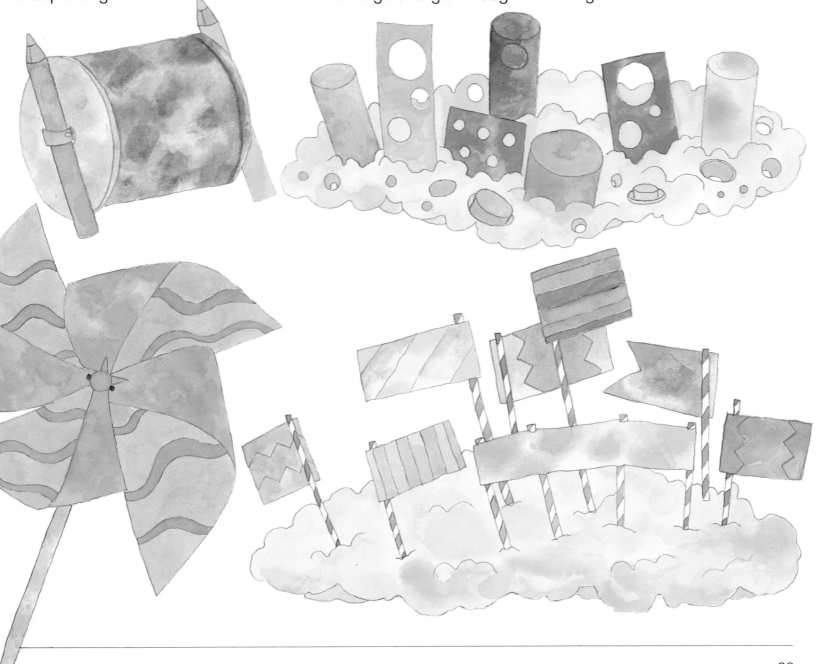

Mobiles

As well as making these for fun, they are also a pleasure to look at. An older child can be encouraged to make one for any babies in the family.

Cut out some shapes from card or coloured paper. (You can buy coloured foil wrapping paper and stick this onto the card so that it catches the sunlight, or decorate the card with bright colours or a collage.)

Thread the shapes with cotton and hang them from threaded triangles of drinking straws, or two coat hangers tied together. To balance properly, the shapes need to be tied to both ends and/or to the centre of the hangers.

Papier-mâché

Half-fill a washing-up bowl with wallpaper paste and cut up some small strips of newspaper. Smear the object that you want to make a model from with vaseline. Dip the strips of newspaper, one at a time, into the paste and lay the strips over the model base until it is covered with several layers of paper. Leave to dry.

A Paper Plate
Grease the top of an old china plate with vaseline. Cover the top of the plate with papier-mâché strips. When dry, trim the edges with a pair of scissors and remove the china plate from underneath.

A Mask
Grease half an inflated balloon and cover that half with papier-mâché. Allow to dry, then burst the balloon and remove it.
   Trim the edges of the mask. Cut out the eye holes and paint on the decorations. You could also glue on some wool or fur bits for hair. Make two small holes on either side of the mask and thread through some elastic to tie the mask in place.

Paper Animals
Completely grease an inflated balloon and cover it with papier-mâché. When dry, glue on cardboard legs, ears and tail, and paint.

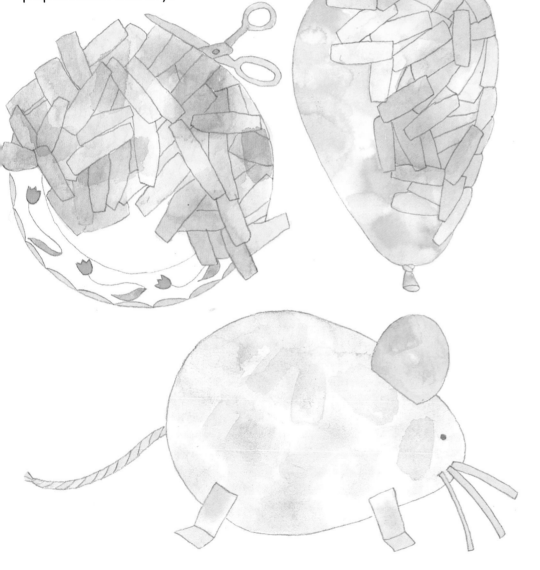

Models

Making Solid Models

Tear up newspaper into small pieces and mash it into a pulp in a bowl of wallpaper paste. Using a handful at a time, squeeze out excess water and mould it into the shape you want, like clay. Leave to dry overnight and paint.

A Model Village

You will need a number of cardboard boxes of various sizes.

Draw a ground plan of a village onto a piece of stiff card. (You could cut out the bottom or side of a large cardboard box for this.) Paint in the roads, and green for grass fields, and so on.

Shops can be made from smaller boxes placed on their sides. Make the open ends the entrances so that dolls can go in and out. Magazine pictures can be stuck to the sides of the boxes as decoration.

Details

Paint on a pond, or use a piece of blue paper or tissue paper, and shape some ducks out of small pieces of dough or plasticine.

Bus stops or traffic lights can be made from pieces of paper glued to lolly-pop sticks and stuck into lumps of plasticine to make the bases.

Garage petrol pumps can be made from plasticine or matchboxes. Put a display outside the greengrocer's shop. The fruit and vegetables can be made from small pieces of plasticine or screwed-up bits of tissue paper. Put them in trays made from matchboxes.

A play house

Use a large cardboard box from an electrical shop (such as a refrigerator or washing-machine box). You can either leave the box whole, and simply cut a door in one side and a window in another. Or, cut off the top and bottom and open out the four sides. Cut two windows in the sides and stand it upright in the corner of a room. Prop one end against the wall, or tape it to the wall if possible, but leave the other end open to act as a doorway. You could drape an old sheet over the top as a roof, and use smaller boxes for furniture.

An obstacle course

You can make this for dolls or, if you have the space, for children.

For dolls, use cardboard boxes, matchboxes and scraps of material. For children use chairs, stools, cushions, cardboard boxes, old sheets or rugs and pieces of newspaper.

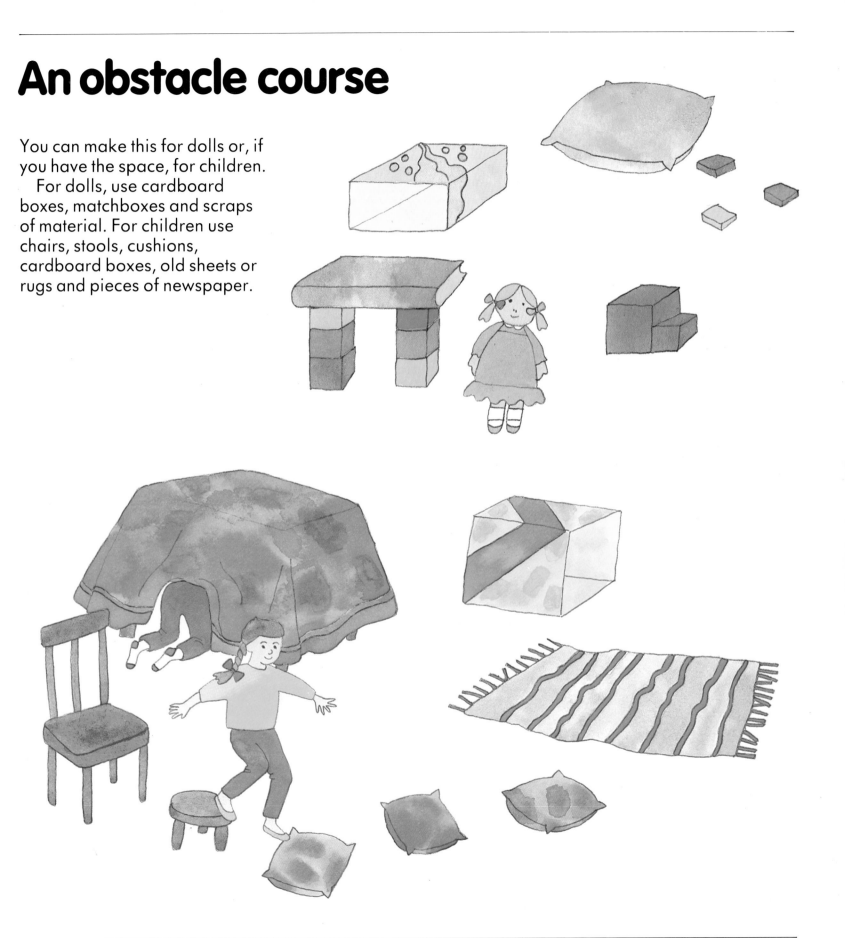

A doll's house

Cut off the tops of four cardboard boxes and glue them together to make the four rooms of a 'house'. (Cardboard wine boxes tend to be a standard size, so try your local off-licence.) Add a touch of realism by cutting out windows and doorways to connect one room with another.

Decorate the boxes with scraps of wallpaper or pieces from a discarded wallpaper-sample book. Furnish the rooms with objects from your art box. Some ideas are shown in the illustrations below and on the opposite page.

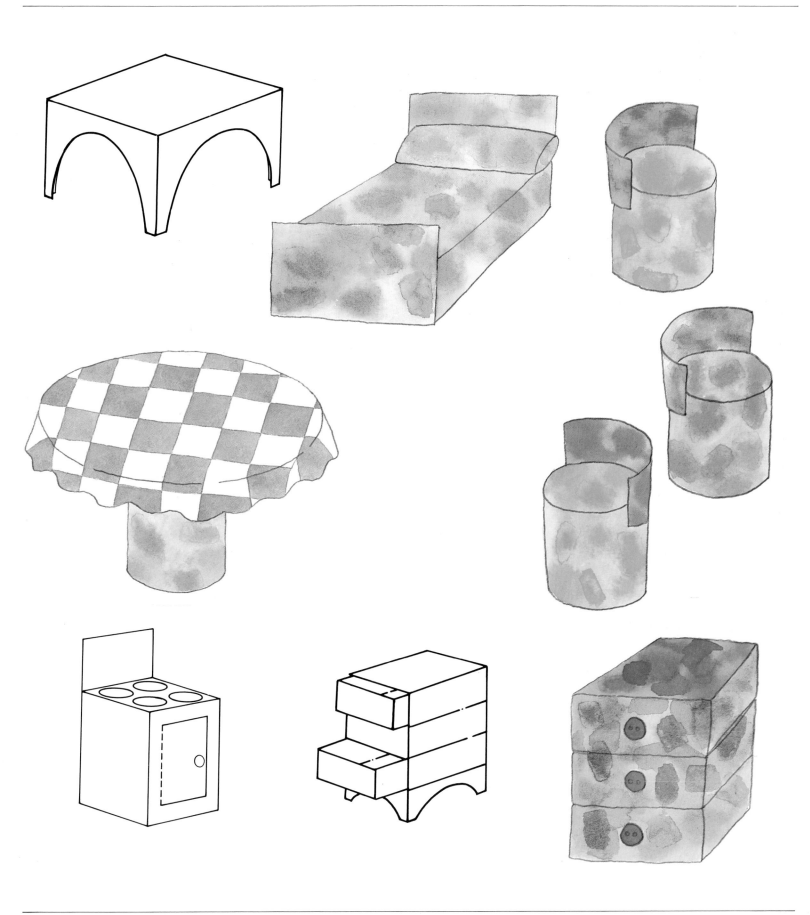

Threading and tying

Shoe Lacing

Draw a large boot onto a piece of card, or trace over the outline of the drawing shown here. Punch holes in the top of the boot and practise threading and tying shoe laces, as with an ordinary shoe.

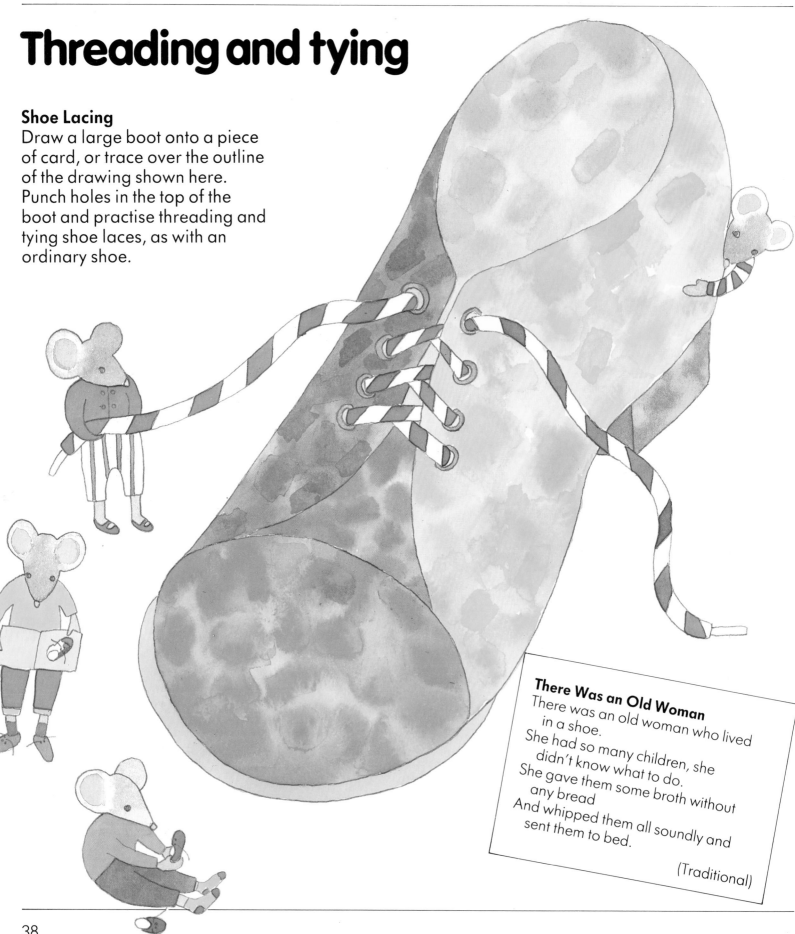

There Was an Old Woman

There was an old woman who lived in a shoe.
She had so many children, she didn't know what to do.
She gave them some broth without any bread
And whipped them all soundly and sent them to bed.

(Traditional)

Threading

1 Cut out a simple shape from a firm piece of cardboard, then cut or punch holes large enough for shoelaces to be threaded through to make a pattern.

2 Trace the shape of your child's name onto a card with punched holes. Thread through the holes with coloured shoelaces.

3 Glue a picture with a clear outline onto a piece of card. Punch large holes all around the edge of the picture (about ½ cm or ¼ inch apart). Help your child to stitch round the picture with a bodkin (a large blunt needle) and wool.

4 Take some cotton reels, or yoghurt pots with holes cut in the bottom, and thread them onto string to make a snake. (Make knots in the string to keep the yoghurt pots apart.)

Older children can thread macaroni (or other types of hollow pasta), pieces of coloured straws, foil bottle tops and beads onto long shoelaces.

Woollen Balls

Cut out two circles of card the same size, and make a medium-sized hole in the middle of each. Put the two card rings together and wind a ball of wool through the middle and around the rings.

When the layers of wool nearly fill the centre hole, cut them by sliding the scissors between the two pieces of card. When you have cut the wool all the way round, pull the pieces of card a little way apart and tie a strong piece of wool firmly round the middle. Then remove the cards.

A Woolly Chicken

Make a woollen ball as above. Fold a pipe cleaner in half and hook it through the wool, before you tie it in the middle and remove the card rings. Use a long piece of wool to tie the middle and leave the two ends dangling for the moment.

Make a smaller ball, and tie the middle of this ball with the same piece of wool that you used to tie the larger one. Shape the pipe cleaners into legs, and stick a felt or cardboard beak onto the head.

Weaving

(Packets of gummed, coloured paper are very useful for this activity.)

Cut out four strips of paper (about 2.5 cm by 20 cm, or 1 inch by 8 inches) in one colour, and four in a contrasting colour.

Stick one end of each of the first four strips to a piece of card to stop them slipping. Keep them fairly close together. Weave the other four strips across the first ones, as shown.

As a variation to this, try cutting the strips with wavy or jagged edges, or use more paper strips.

For Older Children

Make a simple weaving loom from an old shoe box. Punch six holes in either end of the box. Thread a piece of wool through the holes as shown and knot the ends firmly to keep the wool in place. (This is called the 'warp').

Now wind a differently-coloured piece of wool length-wise around a piece of card, leaving approximately 20 cm (8 inches) hanging free. Weave the card through the warp, as shown. Cut the cardboard to remove the finished piece of weaving from the frame.

Woodwork

Tools and Equipment

Collect pieces of scrap wood, a hammer, nails (1 inch, 1½ inch or 2 inch, or metric equivalents), sandpaper, glue, a saw, file, screwdriver, screws, screw hooks and eyes, wooden wheels (or bottle tops), a wooden board (thick enough to work on without the nails piercing the floor) and a vice (especially useful when sawing).

If possible, try to provide small versions of proper tools for your child, rather than buying a play tool kit. Toy tools are frustrating to use and are not a good investment.

Using Tools

Children rarely hurt themselves if they've been shown how to use tools properly, so it's worthwhile first spending a few minutes demonstrating each new tool.

Explain how to hammer in nails. Tap gently at first, then remove your fingers and bang hard. Use potatoes to practise on if wood is too hard.

Practise sawing on thick corrugated card. Develop a rhythm—repeating:
  'Saw up Slowly,
  then down slowly.'

Teach your child to respect their tools by cleaning them and putting them away after use.

Ideas for Things to Make

1. Toys: Robots, ships, lorries, trains, etc. Let the shape of the wood guide you.

2. Sculptures and collages— don't forget to use the shavings and sawdust too.

3. Wool winder: Tap several nails at random into a board, then wind wool round them to make a pattern.

4. Hammer patterns: Make a pattern of holes by hammering a large nail or spike a little way into a piece of wood.

5. Toy-tidier: Sandpaper a piece of wood and screw a row of hooks into it. (You will then need to fix the tidier to a wall or door for your child.) You can use the tidier to hang up bags of bricks or paints, and other toys.

Exploring further

2

Around the house

Explain how the electricity meter works—switch on one or two appliances and watch the dial react. Take this opportunity to warn your child of the dangers of electricity; explain about not touching loose wires, or sockets, and not meddling with appliances.

Trace the route the water takes through your house by following the pipes.

Demonstrate how the radiators work. Hold some strips of paper above a radiator and watch them flutter as the warm air blows them up. Where is the air hotter—above or below the heater?

Use the telephone—listen to the different tones (for the engaged sound dial your own number). Try phoning the telephone services, such as the weather forecast, dial-a-disc, or the bedtime story.

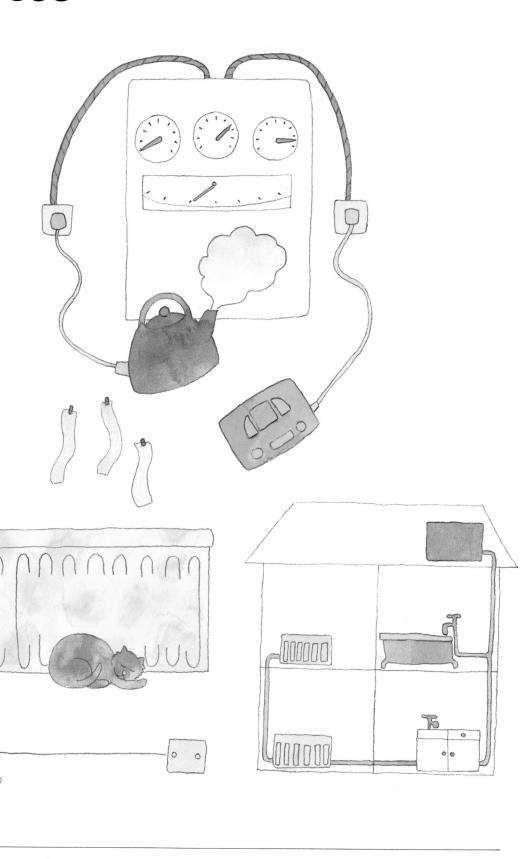

Cooking

Explain to your child about always washing their hands before touching food.

Give your child practice in all the various cooking tasks—weighing, counting, chopping (use a bluntish knife), coring, peeling, grating, mixing, stirring, rolling, etc.

Begin by letting your child help you with part of the recipe. Then, as their interest and powers of concentration grow he or she can gradually learn to prepare a complete dish. Older children can be shown how to use electrical appliances.

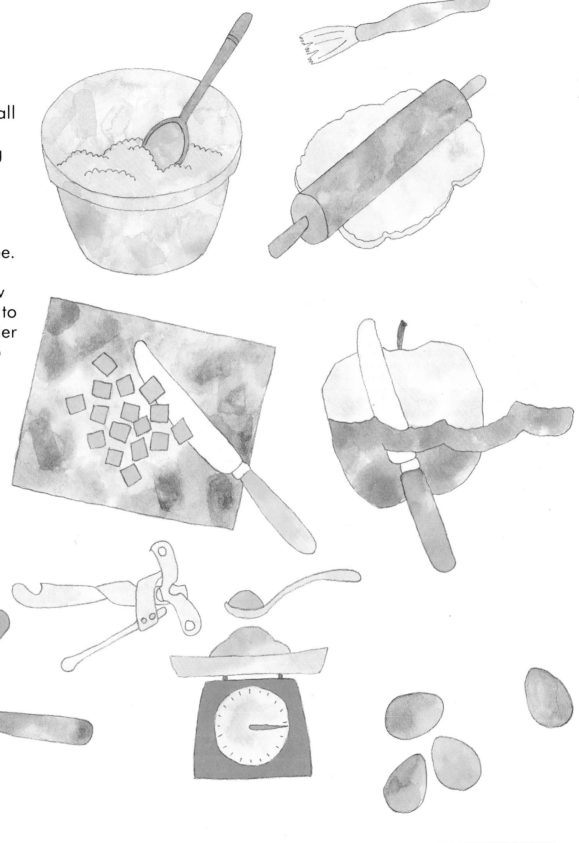

Beginners' recipes

Choose things that are quick yet fun to make.

1 Sandwiches: Experiment with different fillings to learn which flavours go well together. This may lead to some enjoyable tea parties.

Try: Marmite, sardines, cucumber, tomatoes, boiled egg (sliced or mashed with salad cream), cheese, pickle, salami, cottage cheese, grated carrot, liver paté, chopped celery or apple, peanut butter, honey, pineapple, banana (mashed).

2 Scrambled eggs: Melt a knob of butter in a saucepan. Beat together one egg and one tablespoon of milk and pour into the pan.

Cook gently, stirring continuously until the egg mixture sets.

As a variation, try adding one tablespoon of cottage cheese just before the egg sets.

3 Fillings for pancakes, pizzas, baked potatoes and omelettes: Use mushrooms, onions, cucumber, tomato, cooked or grated vegetables, cheese, egg (scrambled or boiled), prawns, chicken, ham, parsley, curry paste, etc.

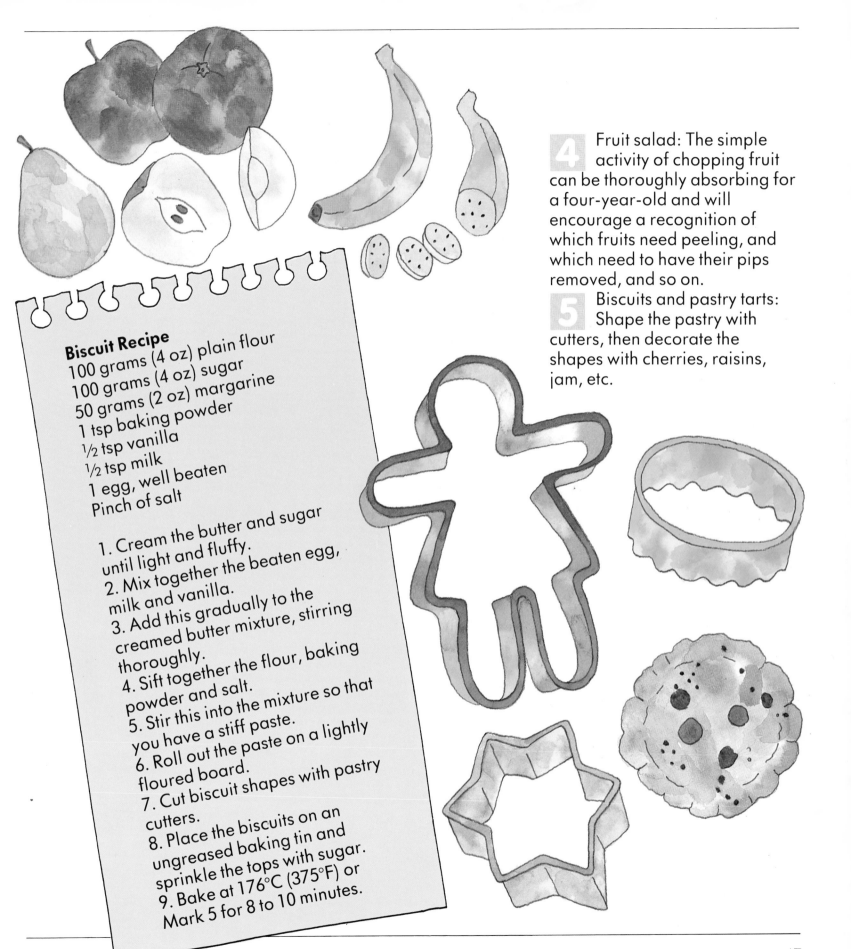

4 Fruit salad: The simple activity of chopping fruit can be thoroughly absorbing for a four-year-old and will encourage a recognition of which fruits need peeling, and which need to have their pips removed, and so on.

5 Biscuits and pastry tarts: Shape the pastry with cutters, then decorate the shapes with cherries, raisins, jam, etc.

Biscuit Recipe

100 grams (4 oz) plain flour
100 grams (4 oz) sugar
50 grams (2 oz) margarine
1 tsp baking powder
1/2 tsp vanilla
1/2 tsp milk
1 egg, well beaten
Pinch of salt

1. Cream the butter and sugar until light and fluffy.
2. Mix together the beaten egg, milk and vanilla.
3. Add this gradually to the creamed butter mixture, stirring thoroughly.
4. Sift together the flour, baking powder and salt.
5. Stir this into the mixture so that you have a stiff paste.
6. Roll out the paste on a lightly floured board.
7. Cut biscuit shapes with pastry cutters.
8. Place the biscuits on an ungreased baking tin and sprinkle the tops with sugar.
9. Bake at 176°C (375°F) or Mark 5 for 8 to 10 minutes.

Cherry Buns

25 grams (1oz) glacé cherries
100 grams (4 oz) self-raising flour
50 grams (2 oz) margarine
50 grams (2oz) sugar
1 beaten egg

1. Count out ten paper baking cases onto a baking tray.
2. Wash the cherries.
3. Rub the margarine into the flour with your fingertips.
4. Thoroughly stir in the sugar and the cherries, and then the beaten egg.
5. Put a small spoonful of the mixture into each of the ten paper cases.
6. Let your child scrape the bowl!
7. Bake at 176°C (375°F) or Mark 5 for 15 minutes.

Having a Picnic

Make a picnic and let your child choose the food. You don't have to go further than the living room to eat it, the fun is in preparing the snacks and packing the bags.

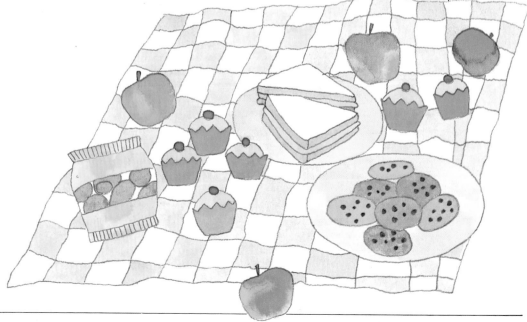

More about food

Where Does Food Come From?
Many children are surprised to learn that peas actually grow in pods on a plant, and that apples grow on trees; that carrots are roots; that milk comes from cows and eggs from chickens.

Have some illustrations of animals, food and food production in the kitchen when you are talking about food.

When you're cooking, let your child see the vegetables before you chop them up, and the meat or fish before you cook it.

Try making some things you would normally buy pre-prepared in packets:

Cheese

1. Leave a little milk out of the fridge until the curds and whey separate.
2. Hang the curds in a bag made of clean linen (e.g. a clean handkerchief), so that the whey can drain away completely. Squeeze out any remaining moisture from the curds.
3. Add a little salt to taste if necessary.

Orange Juice

This can easily be made by squeezing fresh oranges.

Yoghurt

1. Sterilize a vacuum flask, either by immersing it in boiling water or by using a sterilizing solution.
2. Heat 600 ml (1 pint) of sterilized milk to 43°C (110°F)—approximately blood heat, or boil 600 ml (1 pint) of pasteurized milk and leave it to cool to the above temperature.
3. Add a tablespoon of natural yoghurt.
4. Pour the mixture into the vacuum flask, seal it and leave for 6 hours.
5. Transfer the mixture from the flask to a sterilized bowl. Cover and place in fridge for 3 to 4 hours to cool and thicken.

Flavour your yoghurt with chopped fruit, nuts, jam, dessicated coconut, honey, etc.

Coleslaw
Finely chop:
¼ white cabbage
1 small onion
1 large carrot
1 dessert apple

Mix together with salad cream.

Tomato Soup
Place in a saucepan:
15 grams (½ oz) flour
15 grams (½ oz) butter
300 ml (½ pint) milk
200 grams (8 oz) tinned tomatoes
Pinch of salt and pepper

Heat the ingredients, stirring continuously. Bring to boil, cover and simmer for 10 minutes.

As a variation, try adding a chopped onion to the ingredients.

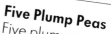

Five Plump Peas
Five plump peas in a pea-pod pressed,
One grew and two grew and so did all the rest.
Grew and grew and grew and grew,
And grew and never stopped.
Till they grew so plump and portly
That the pea-pod popped!

(Traditional)

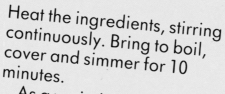

Know your body

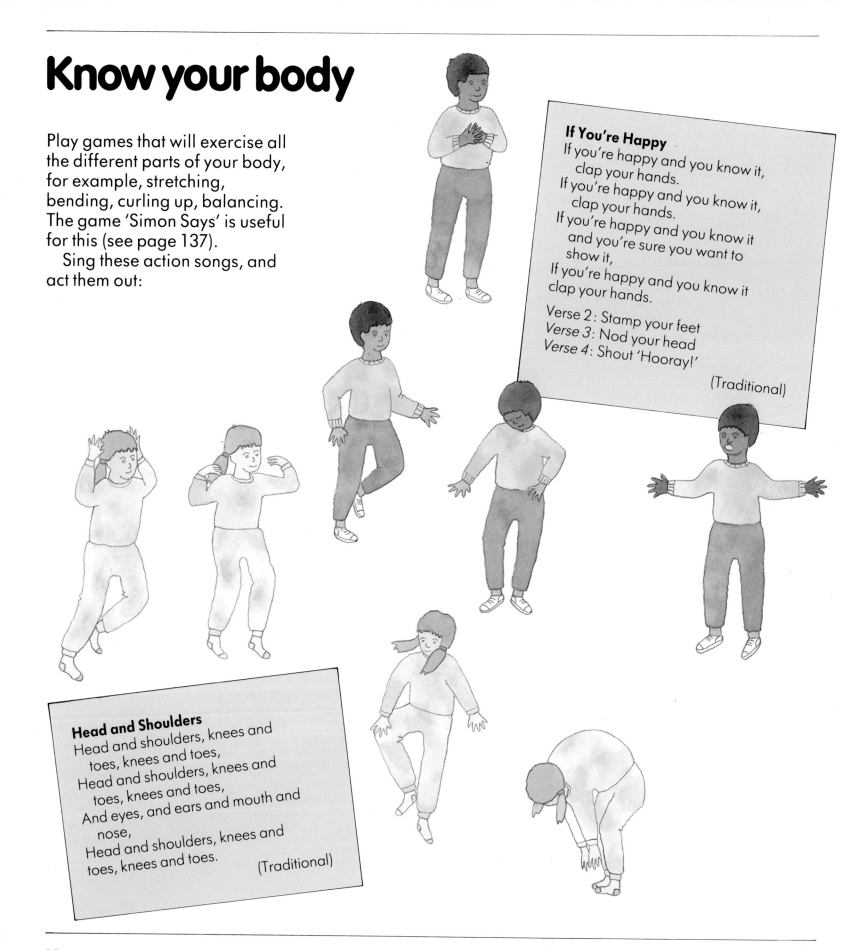

Play games that will exercise all the different parts of your body, for example, stretching, bending, curling up, balancing. The game 'Simon Says' is useful for this (see page 137).

Sing these action songs, and act them out:

If You're Happy
If you're happy and you know it, clap your hands.
If you're happy and you know it, clap your hands.
If you're happy and you know it and you're sure you want to show it,
If you're happy and you know it clap your hands.

Verse 2: Stamp your feet
Verse 3: Nod your head
Verse 4: Shout 'Hooray!'

(Traditional)

Head and Shoulders
Head and shoulders, knees and toes, knees and toes,
Head and shoulders, knees and toes, knees and toes,
And eyes, and ears and mouth and nose,
Head and shoulders, knees and toes, knees and toes.

(Traditional)

One Finger, One Thumb
One finger, one thumb keep moving,
One finger, one thumb keep moving,
One finger, one thumb keep moving,
We'll all be merry and bright.

(Increase each verse by one part
of the body until you reach the
final verse)

One finger, one thumb, one arm,
   one leg, one nod of the head,
   stand up, sit down, keep moving,
One finger, one thumb, one arm,
   one leg, one nod of the head,
   stand up, sit down, keep moving,
One finger, one thumb, one arm,
   one leg, one nod of the head,
   stand up, sit down, keep moving,
We'll all be merry and bright.
                                   (Traditional)

Making Comparisons

Compare parts of the human body, such as hands, feet, eyes and nose, with the different shapes found among animals and birds.

The Senses

Fill an egg box with six ingredients that have easily identifiable tastes or smells (for example, mustard, salt, cocoa, sugar, honey, grapefruit, pepper, tomato sauce, mashed banana, grated cheese, orange, onion, peppermint, cotton wool soaked in vinegar). Make six holes in the lid of the egg box, big enough to put a finger through. Then tape the lid over the box, so that the ingredients are hidden. (You could also use six yoghurt pots with paper lids.)

Tell your child to dip a finger into each section in turn and taste it with their eyes closed. Can they guess what it contains? (NB: Have a glass of drinking water handy!)

For other games using the senses, see:

Listening – pages 118-119
Observation – pages 88-94
Touching – page 140

Playing with water

Children love water and will take every opportunity to play with it. Put a board across the end of your bath and put some of the following items on it:

1 Squeezy bottles, milk cartons, and a plastic toy teapot (pierce holes in the sides of one of these). Use to make air bubbles and for pouring.

2 Pipes, metal rings, sprays, sieves and funnels. Use for pouring water through them.

3 Lengths of tubing, such as plastic straws. Use to siphon water from one type of container to another.

4 Sponges, tissue paper, corks, cotton reels, spoons and plastic toys. Use for floating and sinking.

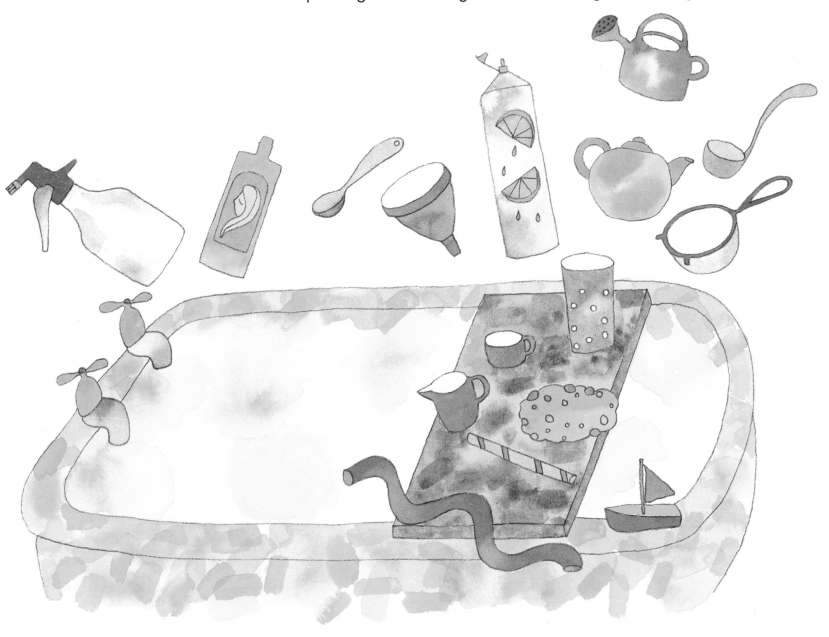

Water games

Water Games

1 Blowing detergent bubbles. Use plastic rings to blow through, or plastic straws cut diagonally at one end.

2 Add a few drops of cooking oil to a bowl of water and swirl it around to make patterns.

3 Playing with ice cubes. Watch them melt; drop them into cups of water and watch them float and crack.

4 Find two containers which hold the same amount of liquid but are different in shape—one taller and narrower than the other. Ask your child which holds the most water – the answer given will probably be the taller. Demonstrate that they both hold the same amount by filling them up and then pouring the water from each one in turn into a measuring jug.

Bottles of Water
Water in bottles,
Water in pans,
Water in kettles,
Water in cans—
It is always the shape
Of whatever it's in,
Bucket or kettle,
Or bottle or tin.

(Rodney Bennett)

Weighing

Make your own balance. Tie a margarine tub to each end of a coat hanger. Make sure the pieces of string are equal in length and the tubs are hung at the same level. Hang up the hanger, using a longer piece of string.

Weigh a number of different items of varying sizes. You can then introduce words such as heavy, heavier, light and lighter.

Make sure that it is not always the larger objects which are heavy and the small ones which are light.

Using a Scale
(Think metric—your child will at school.)

Look at the weights given on food packets in the kitchen cupboard and check them on a set of scales.

Take two bowls. Weigh out 250 grams of flour and place this in one bowl. Then weigh out 250 grams of rice and put in the other bowl. Which looks the largest quantity, the flour or the rice?

Weigh out the same amounts of other ingredients, such as sugar, tomatoes and peas. Compare the volume of these as well.

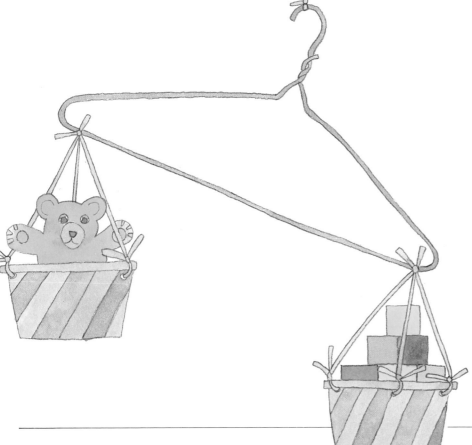

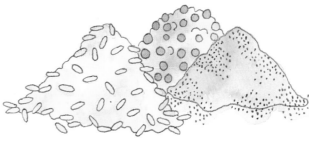

Out of doors

There is so much to see when you leave the house that it would be impossible to cover it all in one book. However, here are a few ideas:

1 Look carefully at building sites. Can you see any cranes, pulleys, wheels? How do they work? What is scaffolding used for?

2 Watch out for dustcarts, buses, fire engines, policemen or women, traffic wardens, traffic lights, pelican and zebra crossings. Talk about their jobs or functions.

3 Visit the local market, the library, shops, and the post office.

4 Look out for billboard advertisements, shop names, road names, shop-door signs ('Push', 'Pull', 'Open', 'Closed') and directions ('Exit', 'Up', 'Down'). Look, too, for symbols that replace words, such as those on road signs, arrows, and pelican crossings.

5 When you get home, talk about what you have seen, using pictures and toys to help. For example: Look at the wheels and axles on toy cars.

Compare a police uniform with other uniforms. Which shop would you go to, to buy objects seen in your house?

Lines and Squares

Whenever I walk in a London street,
I'm ever so careful to watch my
    feet;
And I keep in the squares,
And the masses of bears,
Who wait at the corners all ready
    to eat
The sillies who tread on the lines
    of the street
Go back to their lairs,
And I say to them, "Bears,
Just look how I'm walking in all
    the squares!"

And the little bears growl to each
    other, "He's mine,
As soon as he's silly and steps on
    a line."
And some of the bigger bears try to
    pretend
That they came round the corner to
    look for a friend;
And they try to pretend that nobody
    cares
Whether you walk on the lines or
    squares.
But only the sillies believe their
    talk;
It's ever so portant how you walk.
And it's ever so jolly to call out,
    "Bears,
Just watch me walking in all the
    squares!"

(A.A. Milne)

59

Things to collect

Bus tickets, shop receipts, shells, coloured pebbles, feathers, autumn leaves, twigs, fir cones, nuts, grasses, seeds and berries (also a good moment to warn your child **not** to taste any berries and to wash their hands after touching them).

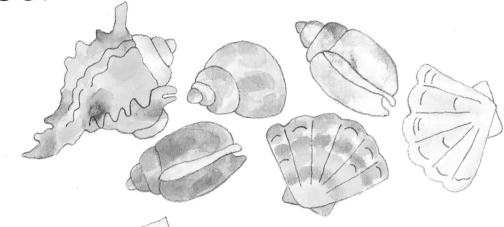

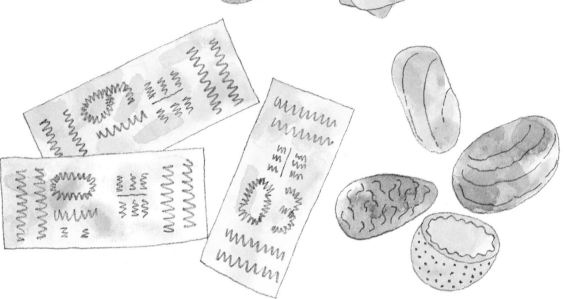

Using your Collections

1 Sort the objects out into small boxes for display.

2 Use them to make collages and models.

3 Take prints by gently rubbing shoe polish onto the backs of leaves and then pressing them onto a sheet of paper.

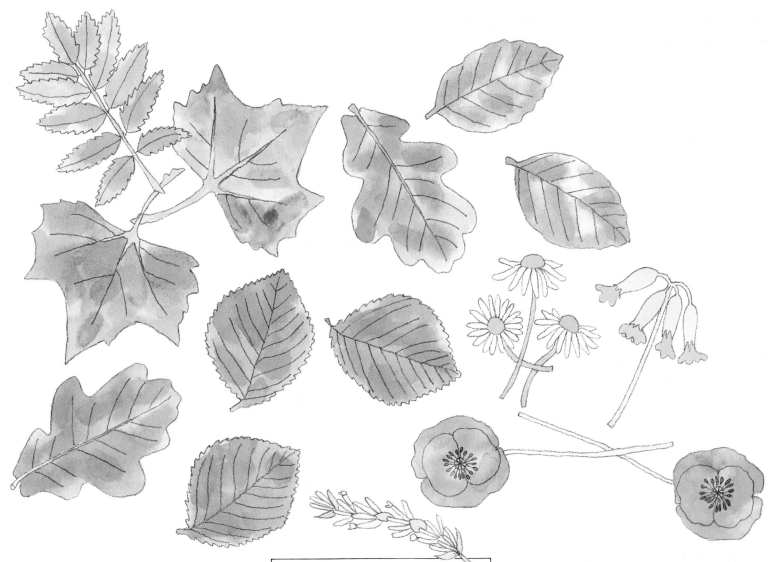

4 Divide the leaves into two groups—deciduous (from trees that shed their leaves in winter) and evergreens (from trees which keep their leaves throughout the winter).

5 Put some bare twigs into a vase to be used as stems for paper flowers. Alternatively, loosely weave them together and wind pieces of differently-coloured wool around them to make a sculpture.

Lavender's Blue
Lavender's blue, dilly dilly,
Lavender's green,
When I am King, dilly, dilly,
You shall be Queen.

(Traditional)

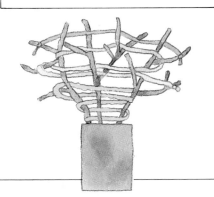

6 Take some flowers from the garden (do not pick wild flowers as many types of wild flower are now becoming extremely rare), and put them between pieces of blotting paper. Pile up some heavy books on top and leave them to press flat.

7 If you have fresh lavender in your garden, collect a bunch of it and hang it up to dry. Then crush it up in the middle of a square of cotton and tie up the corners with ribbon to make a lavender bag.

Learn about growing

Look at some seeds which have wings. Explain how the wind helps to spread them so they can find a place to grow.

Illustrate how plants need water by putting some flowers into a clear vase and marking the water level each day.

Illustrate how plants need light by turning a young plant around and watching its shoots grow towards the light.

Cover one leaf on a plant with silver paper to cut it off from the light and see what happens.

Growing Beans

Line a glass jar with tissues or blotting paper. Place a few runner-bean seeds or broad beans between the glass and the paper so that you can see them through the sides of the glass. Fill the jar with water and keep it in a warm place. The beans will grow some roots first, and then shoots.

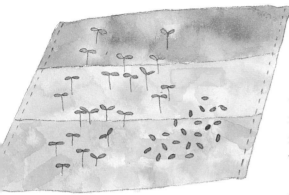

Growing Cress

Place a damp tissue or piece of cotton wool in a saucer and sprinkle it with a few cress seeds. Keep them damp and warm.

Think of some alternative pots for your cress—you could use a margarine tub, or even an eggshell—on which you could paint a face.

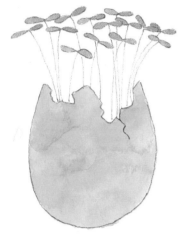

Root Vegetables

Cut the top part off a carrot or a parsnip. Place the sliced edge in a shallow dish of water and watch it sprout new leaves from the top.

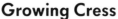

What the Leaves Said
The leaves said, "It's autumn,
Aren't we all gay?"
Scarlet and golden
And russet were they.

The leaves said, "It's winter,
Where are we?"
So they lay down and slept
Under a tree.

The leaves said, "It's spring,
And here are we,
Opening and stretching
On every tree."

The leaves said, "It's summer,
Each bird has a nest,
We make the shadow
Where they can rest."

(Unknown)

Mary, Mary
Mary, Mary, quite contrary,
How does your garden grow?
With silver bells and cockle shells
And pretty maids all in a row.

(Traditional)

Bean Sprouts

Put some dried mung beans in a jar and stretch a piece of thin flannel firmly over the top. Soak the jar overnight in warm water, then drain and leave it in a sunny place. Keeping the flannel in place, rinse the beans twice a day and watch them grow into bean sprouts. (The sprouts can be lightly fried, or eaten cold on salads.)

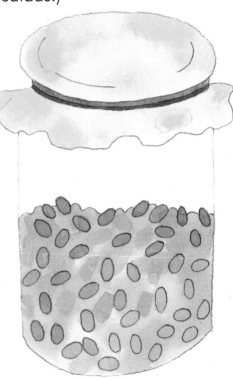

Growing Bulbs

During autumn, buy some bulbs and bulb fibre. Soak the bulb fibre in water and then squeeze out the excess liquid. Put some fibre in a bowl. Set the bulbs upright (they are normally flatter on the bottom) and cover them with the rest of the fibre, pressing it down quite firmly around the bulbs. Keep the bulbs quite close to the surface.

Put the bowl in a warm, dark cupboard for about two months until the shoots appear above the fibre. Keep the fibre moist, but do not over-water. Once the shoots appear you can put the bowl out in the light.

Pip Plants

You can experiment with growing plants from any kind of fruit pips, for example, grapefruit, apple or orange.

Punch a hole in the bottom of a yoghurt pot and put a few small stones inside. Fill the rest of the pot with soil and plant a few fresh pips inside it. Stand the pot in a saucer and keep the soil moist and away from direct sunlight until the seeds sprout.

Don't forget to label the pots if you use more than one type of seed.

Observing animals

As well as looking at animals themselves, it is fun to look for the signs that show where they have been.

Footprints
Look for footprints in mud, sand or snow, and see if you can work out which animal they belong to. For example, a fox's tracks are like a dog's. They zig-zag, as the fox places its hind feet in the holes left by its forefeet.

A sparrow hops along on both feet, so its prints are in pairs.

A duck's tracks show its webbed feet, and the fact that it points its toes inwards as it waddles along.

As a rabbit runs, it puts its large hind feet in front of its small forefeet.

Animal homes

Look for holes, nests and webs. But do not go too close if it seems as if the animal may still be using the home.

You may find a fox's den or a badger's sett under tree roots; or a rabbit's burrow in a grassy bank. Look, too, for squirrels' nests (called 'dreys') in the branches of trees.

Look for birds' nests in trees and hedges. Don't disturb them during the spring or summer, but if you find an abandoned nest in the winter have a look to see how it is made. In the spring, you may also see birds flying to their nests with their beaks full of straw, tissue paper and other nesting materials.

If you find a spider's web, see if you can spot its owner lurking under a leaf by one corner. You may also see a 'spider's nursery'—a tightly woven area of web between two grassy stalks where the spider's eggs are laid.

In the summer you may see 'cuckoo spit' on the stems of plants and grass. These white blobs of froth are the home of the larvae of the froghopper bug. It wraps the froth around itself for protection.

Feeding signs

Look for chewed pine cones and opened nuts on the ground under trees. Hazel nuts opened by squirrels are cracked in half, whereas mice nibble uneven holes in nuts to get at the kernel

caterpillars and snails. Look for leaves that have been chewed. Some leaves have white or brown markings winding over the surface. The markings are made by leaf miners (the grubs of moths or flies), which eat the leaves from inside.

Look, too, at animals and insects as they collect their food. For example, ducks dive head down to search through the weeds. Butterflies and bees gather nectar from flowers. Ants scurry back to their nest with bundles of food.

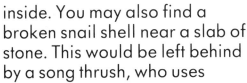

inside. You may also find a broken snail shell near a slab of stone. This would be left behind by a song thrush, who uses

stones to crack open the snail shells to get at the snail inside. Spiders, too, often leave behind the remains of flies unlucky enough to get caught in their webs.

Leaves provide food for many small creatures, such as

Looking at birds

Try to learn to recognize some of the most common species—blackbirds, starlings, sparrows, robins, magpies, wagtails, wrens, thrushes, tits and finches.

Encourage your child to put food out for them on a window ledge, but try to include things like dried fruit, seeds and nuts as well as just bread. Many birds like bacon rind and cheese as well.

Bird Talk
"Think . . . ," said the Robin,
"Think . . . ," said the Jay,
Sitting in the garden,
Talking one day.
"Think about people—the
    way they grow:
They don't have feathers
    at all, you know.
They don't eat beetles
They don't grow wings,
They don't like sitting
    on wires and things."
"Think . . . ," said the Robin,
"Think . . . ," said the Jay.
"Aren't people funny
    to be that way?"
(Aileen Fisher)

An Owl Flew Down
An owl flew down
    from an old oak tree,
"Twiddle-a-whoo," quoth he.

"O little brown mouse
Come out of your house
I'd like you to come to tea, to tea,
I'd like you to come to tea."

Out of a hole in the oak tree bole,
A little mouse looked to see
Who asked her to come to tea, to tea,
Who asked her to come to tea.

"You're quite absurd, you silly old bird,
To ask me to come to tea.
The tea you would eat is me, is me,
The tea you would eat is me!"
(Unknown)

Making a bird table

As an alternative to the window ledge you could try making a hanging bird table. Nail or glue four sticks of wood horizontally round the edges of a piece of

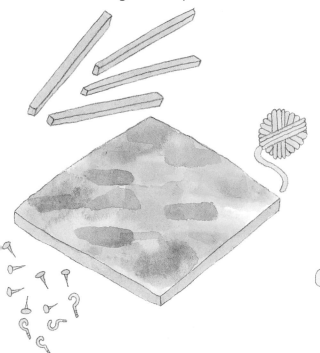

board about 30 cm (12 inches) square. Fix a hook into each corner, then tie string to the hooks and hang the board outside your window.

You can also hang food from your tray. If you have an empty half of a coconut shell, drill a hole in it and thread it with a piece of string. Then pour some melted fat inside and let it set. You could also put out pieces of fresh coconut and watch the birds peck it away from the shell. Another favourite is *unsalted* peanuts, inside a

plastic or wire mesh bag. Don't forget to put out some water; use a shallow dish that is unbreakable.

In spring, you could put out nesting materials, such as scraps of cotton, string, small twigs, and hair from hairbrushes. Put these inside a mesh bag and hang it from the bird table.

Keeping pets

The chance of looking after a living creature is very rewarding for young children. Not only do they learn about the animal and its life, but also how to care for it.

Some small wild animals and insects can be kept for a few days without much harm, for example, garden snails, caterpillars, spiders and worms. Keep them in containers which let in air, but will also prevent them from escaping, such as small fish tanks or jars, sealed firmly with netting or paper covered with lots of pin holes.

Caterpillars

Caterpillars can be collected from hedges and the leaves of flowers throughout the summer. Remember not to remove them from the leaf on which you find them and to give them fresh leaves of the same kind every day.

After a time, the caterpillar will build itself a cocoon (called a chrysalis). Then, a couple of weeks later, it will emerge as a butterfly or moth and will want to fly away. Do not try to keep butterflies or moths or they will soon die.

Some caterpillars and most butterflies have beautiful markings. You could make a collage of a butterfly from tissue paper. To make the wings identical in size and design, paint the shape of one wing and then fold the paper in half before the paint dries.

The Centipede
The centipede was happy quite,
Until the toad in fun
Said, "Pray, which leg goes after which?"
Which worked his mind to such a pitch,
He lay distracted in a ditch,
Considering how to run.
(Unknown)

Tickle Rhyme
"Who's that tickling my back?"
Said the wall.
"Me," said the small caterpillar,
"I'm learning to crawl."
(Ian Serraillier)

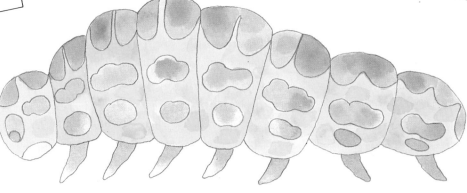

71

Snails and Stick Insects

Snails can be found under stones in fields or gardens and on the side of garden walls during the summer. They should always be kept in a moist atmosphere—put some damp soil in the jar with them. Snails feed mainly at night, so give them some fresh green leaves each evening.

Stick insects can be bought from some pet shops. They are usually fed on privet leaves—but ask the shopkeeper.

Spiders

Spiders can be caught in bushes or in the house. Collect them up in a cardboard box so they are not harmed.

You can only keep a spider for a few days so it will not need feeding, but if you can trap a small fly it will provide the spider with a tasty meal.

Carefully place the spider in a jar that will give it plenty of room, with a little pot inside it containing wet cotton wool. Keep the cotton wool moist.

1. Draw a spiral pattern onto a 20-cm (8-inch) square wooden board.
2. Partially hammer 33 pins into the board as shown below.
3. Starting from the centre and working outward, wind a piece of thread around each of the pins. Do not include the seven outer pins of the spiral.
4. Then wind the thread backward and forward across the outer pins on the board, as shown in the drawing, to make the radiating lines of the web.

Give the spider a small stick with several branches and perhaps it will weave a web for you.

You can make a web of your own on a board using panel pins and cotton:

Worms

Collect one or two worms from a field or garden. If you water a little patch of grassy ground this will often bring worms to the surface.

1 Fill a large jam jar to 2.5 cm (1 inch) from the top with alternate layers of damp sand and soil. Place a few leaves on top and cover the sides of the jar with brown paper so that the worms will burrow near the sides of the glass without being put off by the light.

Put the worms on the top of the leaves and then leave them. After a day or two, remove the brown paper and have a peep at the patterns made by the burrowing worms.

2 Place a worm carefully on a piece of paper and watch it stretching and contracting its body to move itself along.

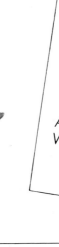

The Frog

Be kind and tender to the Frog,
And do not call him names,
As 'Slimy skin', or 'Polly-wog',
Or likewise 'Ugly James',
Or 'Gape-a-grin', or 'Toad-gone-wrong',
Or 'Billy Bandy-knees':
The Frog is justly sensitive
To epithets like these.
No animal will more repay
A treatment kind and fair;
At least so lonely people say
Who keep a frog (and, by the way,
They are extremely rare).

(Hilaire Belloc)

Tadpoles

First collect some frogspawn in a jar. It can usually be found at the edge of a pond in early summer. Keep the frogspawn in pond water.

Tadpoles need to take oxygen from the water so it is better to put them into a container which has a wide top when you get home. Scoop up plenty of pond weed to put in the container as well, and put in one or two large stones. Later on, as they begin to turn into frogs, the tadpoles will need to climb out of the water to breathe.

Watch the tadpoles as they hatch from the frogspawn. At first, they eat the jelly surrounding their eggs, then tiny animals in the pond water. Keep them supplied with plenty of fresh pond weed and pond water.

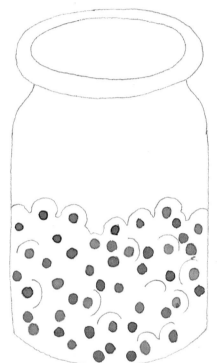

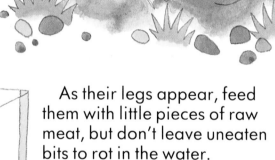

As their legs appear, feed them with little pieces of raw meat, but don't leave uneaten bits to rot in the water.

Once their front legs begin to grow and their tails start to shrink it's time to return them to the pond where they will gradually spend more time out of the water, as they develop into adult frogs.

Whatever the weather

On a Sunny Day

1 To paint a large sun, splodge thick paint onto the centre of a piece of paper and use fingers to paint the rays spreading outwards.

2 Paint on the paths with water, using decorators' brushes.

3 How many things can you think of to cool you down—ice cream, ice-cubes, cold baths, garden hoses . . . . .

4 Study your shadow. When is it shorter or longer? Does it always fall in the same direction? Watch it as you jump, run, dance and pass other people.
Trace someone's shadow onto a large sheet of paper—or paint it in water on the path.

Rainbows

Rainbows are seen when the sun shines through drops of water.

1 Make your own by putting a glass of water on a window sill. You will need a bright sunny day. Place the glass so that the edge just hangs over the edge of the sill. A rainbow should form on the floor. Or, stand with your back to the sun and look through the spray from a garden hose or sprayer.

2 Cut a circle of card. Divide the circle into seven parts, one for each colour of the rainbow. Colour each of the parts as shown in the drawing, and put a pencil through a hole in the middle. Now spin the card.

On a Cloudy Day

1 Make a picture of a cloudy sky using cotton wool glued to the paper for clouds. Develop the theme further by sticking scraps of thick material underneath and drawing heads and feet on them to represent people dressed in warm clothes.

2 Look at the different types of cloud. The wispy 'Mares' tails' usually mean fine weather. Fluffy 'Cumulus' clouds, which look like cotton wool, will mean fine weather if they are small or showers if they are large and grey. Huge patches or 'blankets' of grey or white cloud ('Stratus' cloud) usually mean rain.

When it Rains

1 Hold a thin sheet of paper (so that the surface is flat) out of the window for a few seconds. Bring the paper inside, but keep it flat until the water it has caught has seeped through, then hold it up to a light to see the pattern of the raindrops.

When the Wind Blows

1 Watch the wind blowing the branches of trees, lifting kites, and moving smoke. How many other things can you see that are affected by the wind?

2 Go outside and hold up a wet finger—the side that becomes cold first is the side the wind blows on.

3 Watch the way the clouds move.

2 Talk about what happens to rivers when it rains. Where does all the rainwater from the roofs, roads and hills go to?

In Snow and Ice

1 Collect a jar full of snow. When it melts, how much water is there? More or less then you would have expected?

2 If you can, look at snowflakes through a magnifying glass.
Make your own snowflakes by folding a square of paper into quarters and snipping random shapes out of it.

3 Leave a bucket of water outside on a frosty night so that it freezes. In the morning, make a hole in the middle with a hammer. How thick is the ice? What lies underneath?

4 Talk about how snow is cleared from the roads.

5 Look at footprints in the snow. Compare their sizes. Can you see any belonging to animals or birds?

6 What happens to your body when it's cold outside? Can you see your breath like steam in the cold air? What colour do your cheeks turn?

Make a weather calendar

Use a large piece of thick card as a base and make a set of smaller cards to clip on. Make a small card for:

1 Each of the seven days of the week.

2 Seven different types of weather—sunny, cloudy, showery, foggy, rainy, windy and snowy.

3 Four for each of the seasons.

Your child can help by drawing pictures on the cards to illustrate the words, or you could make up collages from pictures in magazines and catalogues.

Keep the cards in a box, and pin up the correct ones for each day.

The seasons

Make large collage pictures to illustrate the seasons. Use your child's paintings as well as pictures from magazines, and objects like leaves collected on walks.

Tell stories about the seasons, for example, 'Going for a walk in winter'; 'The park in summer'; 'What a squirrel does in the autumn'; 'The robin in springtime'.

Bring out the different features of each season in your stories. For example, in autumn talk about blackberries; squirrels gathering nuts; leaves falling; fog; bonfires.

In winter, talk about animals going into hibernation; frost; snow; bare twigs; long nights; rosy cheeks; Christmas; warm clothes; fires.

In spring—new shoots; lambs; crocuses; daffodils; Easter eggs; umbrellas for showers.

In summer—long days; bees; flowers; strawberries; picnics; trips to the seaside; swimwear; paddling pools; playing outdoors.

Rain
There are holes in the sky
Where the rain gets in
But they're ever so small
That's why rain is so thin.
(Spike Milligan)

Go Wind Go
Go wind go,
Push wind, swoosh.
Shake things, take things,
Make things fly.
Ring things, swing things,
Fling things high.
Go wind go,
Push wind . . . . . whee!
No wind, no!
Not me, not me!
(Lilian Moore)

What to wear

1 Take out a variety of clothes and talk about which clothes are suitable for which kinds of weather. Sort them into piles for summer wear and winter wear, or a trip to the seaside, or a winter holiday.

2 Make paper clothes for all weathers to dress up cardboard dolls (see page 26).

3 Look at pictures of animals' fur and birds' feathers—which animals grow thicker fur in winter? Drop a little water onto a feather to see how waterproof it is.

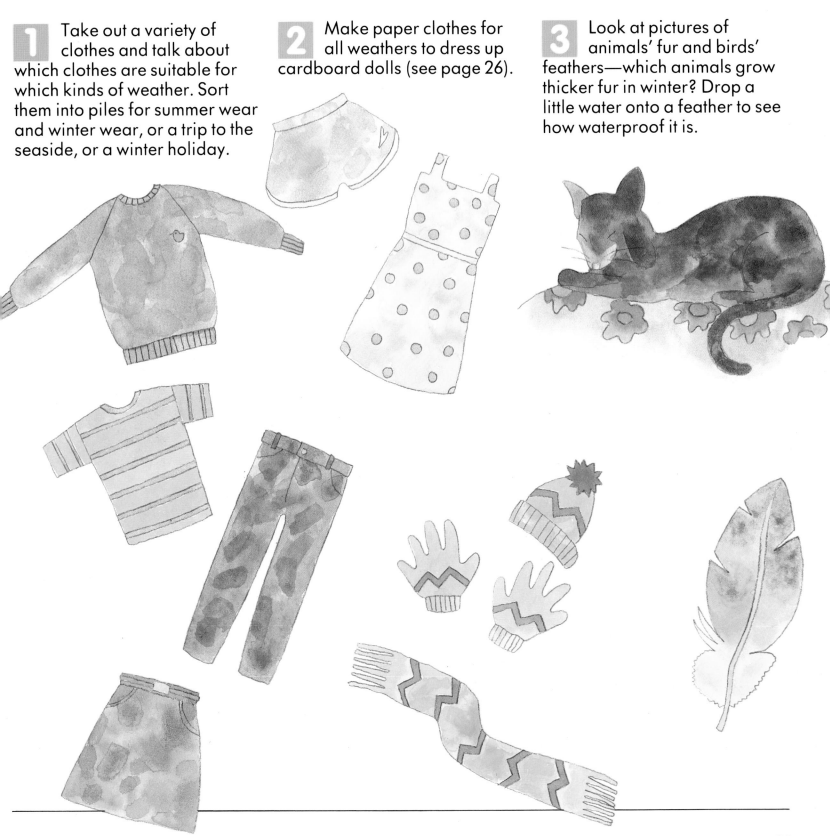

4 Cover three wooden play bricks with white paper, or make three cardboard cubes (see diagram on page 109). On the first cube draw six heads— one on each side. On the second, draw six upper bodies and arms; and on the third, six lower bodies and legs.

Vary the clothing that each drawing shows to make up six people wearing a different outfit. For example: Cotton dress and sun hat; Eskimo type furs; swimsuit and flippers; a uniform; boots and raincoat; working overalls.

Match the correct sides to make up the whole characters, and mix them up, too.

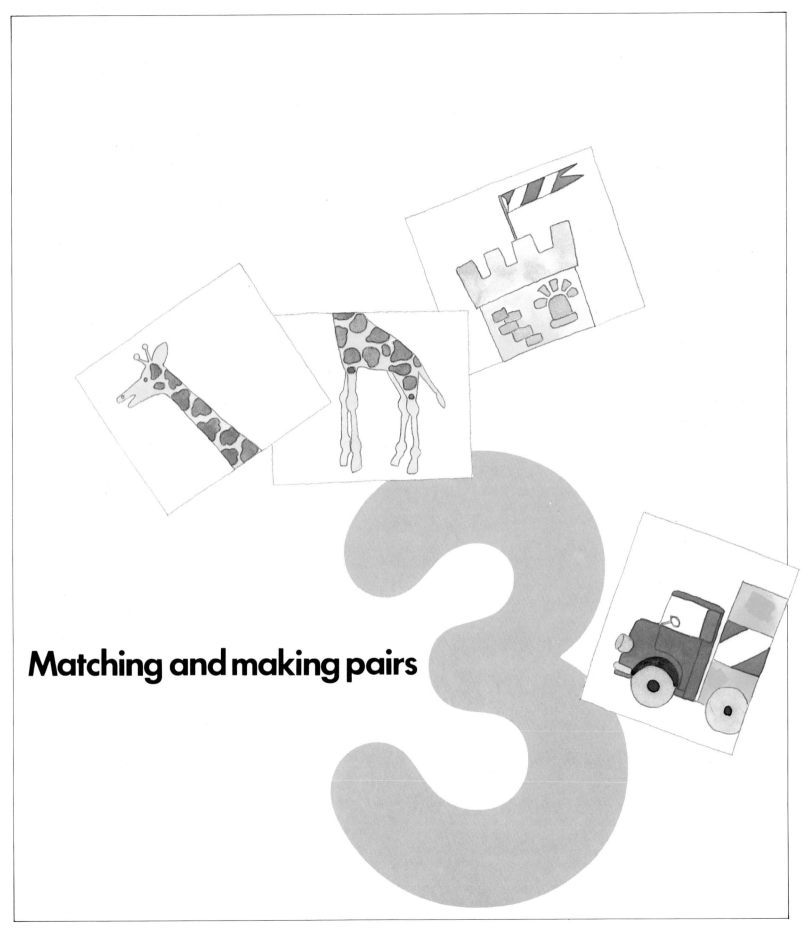

Matching and making pairs

Colour

1 Sort any group of objects into piles according to colour. For example, divide up the washing into dark and light clothes.

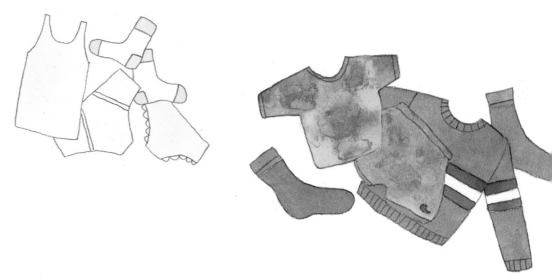

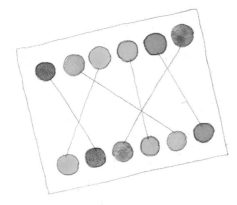

2 Paint six different colours on the left-hand side of a piece of paper and then put the same colours in a different order on the opposite side. Then match up the colours by joining them up with a pencil line. (Encourage you child to work from left to right as a preparation for reading.)

3 Draw two rows of six circles. Colour in the top six yourself but leave the others for your child to colour in matching shades.

4 Collect pictures from magazines. Cut a piece of colour from each picture. Mount the pictures onto card and match the coloured piece to the correct picture.

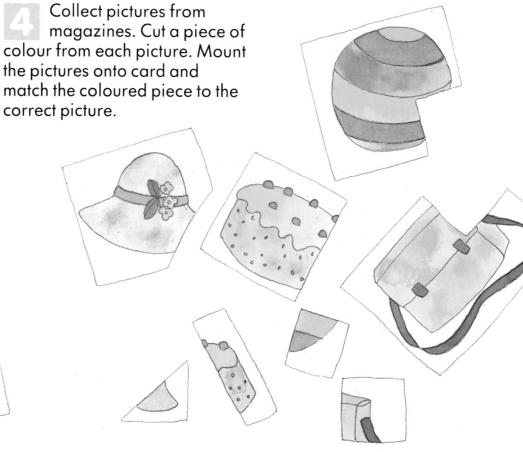

A colour game

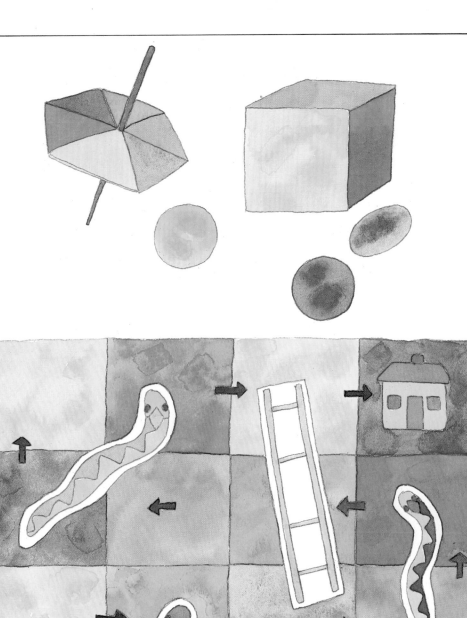

Make a spinner out of a piece of card (see page 109) and divide it into six colours. Or, cover the six sides of a square wooden brick in a different colour for each side. Then divide a large sheet of stiff card into 20 squares. Colour in all the squares using the six colours on the spinner or brick. (Or, you can buy packets of gummed coloured squares and stick these onto the card instead.) Mark the 'Start' and 'Finish' boxes and stick or paint on a few arrows to show which direction the players move in. You will also need some counters.

To play—spin the spinner, or use the brick like a dice, and move your counter to the next square matching the colour the spinner has stopped on. Always move in the direction shown by the arrows. The winner is the first person to reach the 'Home' square by spinning the correct colour.

To make the game more fun, you could paste on some snakes and ladders as well

START

Shapes

1 Cut a piece of fruit in half and point out how each half matches in shape.

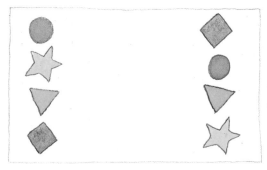

2 Fold a long piece of paper into pleats not less than 5 cm (2 ins) wide. Cut the pleated paper into any shape, but be careful to leave some of the edges on both sides uncut. Open out the paper and you should have a row of identical shapes.

3 Stick some simple shapes onto the left-hand side of a piece of paper (you can buy some boxes of gummed paper shapes, or see page 97 for some examples which you could trace). Stick the same shapes, but in a different order, onto the opposite side of the paper and join up the identical shapes with pencil lines.

4 Find an example of each of the solid shapes shown below and say what the names of the shapes are. Now look for other objects that have similar basic shapes.

5 Draw four objects onto a piece of card. Make them very different in shape—for example, a pencil, a bottle, a cereal packet and a ball. Cut the pictures out. Now make four cards, each one showing a container that fits the shape of each of the objects. Make the shapes very simple, so that it will be easy for your child to match the bag to the object.

Two Little Dicky Birds
Two little dicky birds,
Sitting on the wall,
One named Peter,
The other named Paul.
Fly away Peter, fly away Paul.
Come back Peter, come back Paul.

(Traditional)

Sizes

Does your child understand words that indicate size, such as big, large, small, short, tall and long? Draw or glue pairs of pictures onto a large piece of paper to demonstrate the meaning of big and little, long and short, fat and thin. Talk about the pictures and put circles around the smallest, shortest and thinnest.

1 Make two cards—one bigger and one smaller. Write the words 'bigger' and 'smaller' on the cards—to help non-readers, make each word clearly match the size of the card.

Now take two objects that are the same shape but different sizes, such as a tablespoon and a teaspoon. Put the tablespoon on the 'bigger' card, and the teaspoon on the 'smaller' card. Use a variety of other objects as well, for example, a football and tennis ball; a 2p coin and a 1p coin; a big bowl and a small bowl. Sometimes put the smaller object down first, and sometimes the bigger, and put each pair down separately.

2 Collect several tins or pots of different sizes, each one with a lid. Take the lids off and mix them up. Put the right lid back on the right pot.

3 Collect a number of small objects and sort them into two piles—those that you think will fit into a matchbox and those that won't. Now find an empty matchbox and see if you are right.

4 Take a selection of toys and other objects and sort them into two piles—those that you think would fit through a letterbox and those that won't. Cut a hole the size of a letterbox into the side of a cardboard box. Now try 'posting' the things in your pile.

This game can also be played using holes of different shapes and sizes.

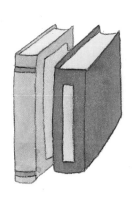

5 Line up a row of books of different heights on a flat piece of wood, or tabletop. Now arrange them in order of height.

Games to play

1 Draw three women, each one a different size and each on a separate sheet of paper. Arrange them in order of size.

2 Draw three potted plants, each one a different size, and arrange these in order.

Mix the two sets together, and then sort them so that the largest woman has the biggest plant, and so on.

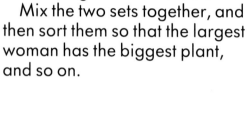

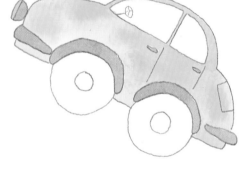
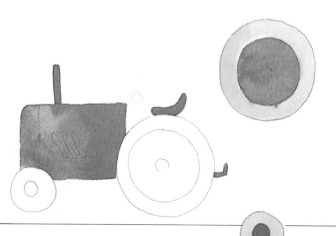

3 Draw three vehicles, all with wheels of different sizes. Colour in the vehicles but not the wheels. Cut out some paper circles to match all the wheel sizes and colour them in to match the right vehicle. Stick the right wheels to the right vehicles.

Goldilocks and the three bears

Cut a sheet of card into 12 pieces. Draw each of the bears on three of the cards; their chairs on three others; their porridge bowls on three others and their beds on the last three. Each time, make one of the drawings large, one medium-sized and one small. Tell the story, holding up the cards as illustrations. Then play with the cards, sorting them by object and then by size.

Things that go together

Shape Matching

Cut out some card templates of basic shapes (some examples are on page 97). Make up some pictures by drawing around the templates on a clean piece of paper. To complete the designs, give your child some ready-made shapes cut out from gummed coloured paper.

To make a game from this project, make up a few pictures on separate pieces of card using the outlines of only six different shapes. Then cut out a set of all the shapes needed to complete all the pictures and colour them in. Make a dice from a piece of firm card (see page 109) with each shape shown on one side of the dice.

Each player is given an outline picture.

The coloured shapes are spread out randomly over the table.

To play—the first player throws the dice. If the shape that falls uppermost on the dice matches one on his or her outline picture, the player picks up the matching piece from the coloured shapes and places it on their card. The winner is the first person to complete a picture.

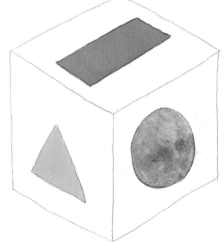

Shadow Matching

Stick 12 clearly-outlined pictures onto thick card and cut them out. (Cheap colouring-in books are a good source for these kinds of pictures.) Take another piece of card and trace around each cut-out. Colour in the shapes with black. Now match the cut-out pictures to the shadow shapes.

Picture Pairs

Build up a collection of pictures of things that can be paired, such as a spider and its web, a telephone and its receiver, and so on. Muddle up all the pictures and then sort them into the correct pairs. You can also do this with real objects—like a knife and fork, cup and saucer, hairbrush and comb, etc.

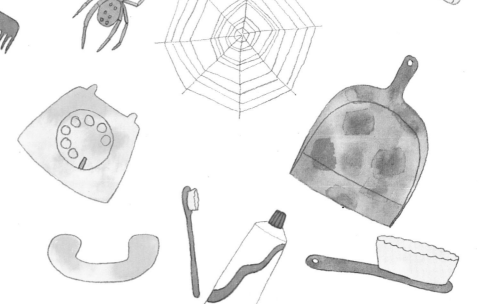

Mix and muddle

1 Make some cards showing the two halves of different pictures, for example, the heads and tails of animals or the tops and bottoms of buildings. Jumble all the cards up then match up the halves.

2 Gather an assortment of shoes, boots and slippers; or cut out pictures of shoes from magazines and mount them onto separate bits of card. Now sort them into pairs, colours or types.

3 Make your own book by folding four sheets of paper in half and stitching firmly down the side of the fold as shown. Cut the pages into three sections, stopping just before you get to the stitching.

Draw two faint pencil lines down each page, about 4 or 5 cms apart (about 2 ins) and always the same distance from the edge. Draw a different figure on each page so that the heads are on the top third, the bodies on the middle third and the legs on the bottom. Use the pencil lines as a guide so that each part of the body is positioned in the same place on every page.

Now you can flip over different sections of each page to make a variety of funny-looking characters.

Jigsaws

Choose a simple picture, for example, from the front of a birthday or Christmas card, the cover of an old scrapbook, or a chocolate-box lid.

Mount the picture onto thick card to make it easier to handle and then let your child study the picture carefully.

Draw a thick border line all round the picture to help identify the edge and corner pieces. Then cut the picture into four pieces (you can increase the number of pieces as your child's skill improves). Try to include something on each piece to give a clue to its position. To cut the edges cleanly use a craft knife or a Stanley knife.

Cut a frame from thick card that will fit around the edge of the picture. Let your child put the pieces together inside the frame so that the pieces won't slide about.

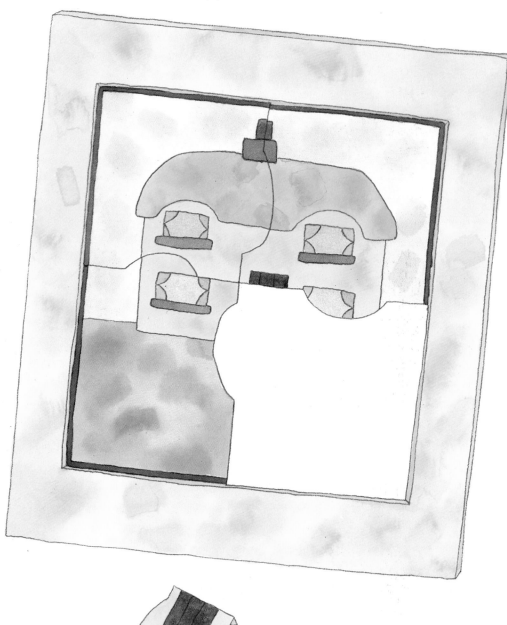

Making your own cards

Cards can be used for all kinds of matching and pairing games. Whether you use letters, numbers or pictures on your cards depends on your child's knowledge and ability. Choose simple shapes and pictures for a young child, and clearly-written numbers, letters and simple words for a child learning to count and read.

There are some suggestions for games on the following pages, but first, here are a few general hints about making cards.

Recommended card size
Make your cards about 8 cm by 6 cm (3 ins by 2¼ ins)—for dominoes these can easily be divided in half.

Designs

1 Shapes—use the shapes shown on the previous page by tracing over them.

2 Pictures—the pictures shown on the next few pages will give you some ideas, and there are some animal pictures you can copy on pages 147–148.

3 Numbers—use only the numbers from 0 to 10 to begin with and write them out clearly.

4 Letters—use lower-case (i.e. small) letters only to begin with, and write them out clearly and boldly.

5 Words (for playing snap) —choose words that your child is learning and use lower-case letters throughout.

Colour Coding

To help your child match up the cards you could use colour coding. For example, make all the cards in one set the same colour, and all the cards in another set a different colour.

Other Uses

When you are making cards for a particular game think of other ways in which they can be used. For example, choose pictures that can be grouped together, such as shoes and socks or hats and coats. Or draw objects that illustrate the words your child is learning to read.

All of the games mentioned on the next four pages can be played using either shape, picture, number or letter cards.

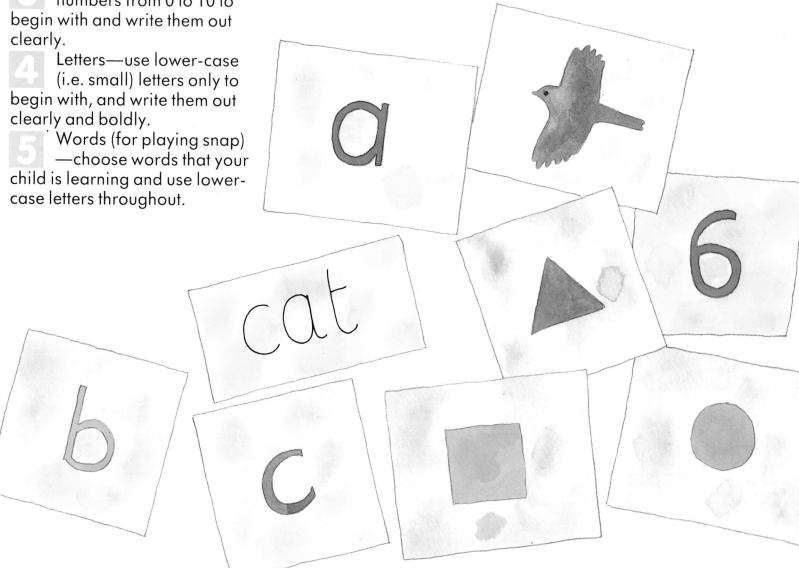

Card games

Pairs

Make a set of 12 pairs of cards (24 cards in all). Scatter them face-downwards on the table.

To play—the first player turns over any two cards. If they are a pair the player picks them up and keeps them. If not, the player must turn them face-downwards again, leaving them in the same position (and trying to remember what was on them). Then it is the turn of the next player. The winner is the person to collect the most pairs.

For young children: To introduce the game to a young child, use only three pairs (six cards) to begin with and gradually increase the number of pairs.

Lotto

This game is for two players. Make 12 pairs of cards (24 in all). Put one card from each pair in a box and shake them up. Lāy six of the other cards face up in front of each player.

To play—each player in turn chooses a card from the box. If the card they have chosen matches one of the cards in front of them they place it on top of the correct card. If not, the card is returned to the box. The winner is the first person to cover their six cards.

Happy Families

Make 24 cards—six sets with four identical cards in each set. Shuffle the cards and deal six to each player. Stack the remainder face-down between the players. The object is to collect complete sets of four identical cards.

To play—the first player asks another player for a card (to match one that they hold in their hand). For example, one player could ask another one for a card with a cat on it.

If the other player has the card they must hand it over immediately to the first player, who then has another turn. If the other player doesn't have the card, the first player takes a card from the stack in the centre and the turn passes to the next player. When a player completes a set, they should place it on the table in front of them.

The game continues until all the sets have been collected. The winner is the player with the largest number of sets.

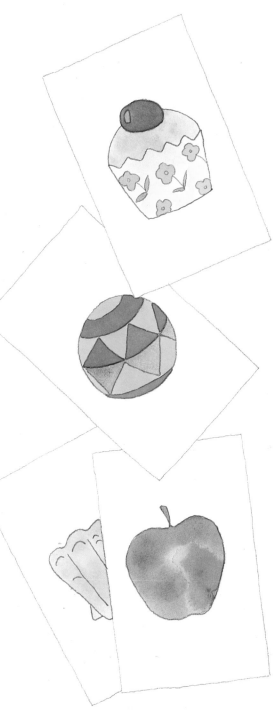

Snap

Make 24 cards—six sets with four identical cards in each set. Shuffle the cards and deal them all out amongst the players, face-downwards so that the players do not know what cards they have.

To play—each player in turn takes a card from the top of their pack and places it face-up on the table. When two identical cards appear together both players must shout 'snap'. The first player to call out wins all the cards that have been put down so far and adds them to the bottom of their own pile.

The winner is either the player who has the most cards at the end of the game, or the one who wins all the cards.

Note: For games of Snap or Happy Families involving more than two players, you may wish to make more than six sets of cards.

Dominoes

Make a set of 28 cards using seven different numbers (or letters or pictures) in the sequence shown opposite. Place all the dominoes face-down on the table. Each player takes eight dominoes, which they can look at. The remainder are left face-down in the centre of the table.

To play—the first player lays down one of their dominoes face-up. If the second player can match one of the pictures with a domino of their own they put that domino down next to the first one. If not, the second player must take a domino from the spare pile, and the turn passes to the first player.

The winner is the first player to have no dominoes left.

1	1	1	2	1	3	1	4	1	5	1	6	1	7
		2	2	2	3	2	4	2	5	2	6	2	7
				3	3	3	4	3	5	3	6	3	7
						4	4	4	5	4	6	4	7
								5	5	5	6	5	7
										6	6	6	7
												7	7

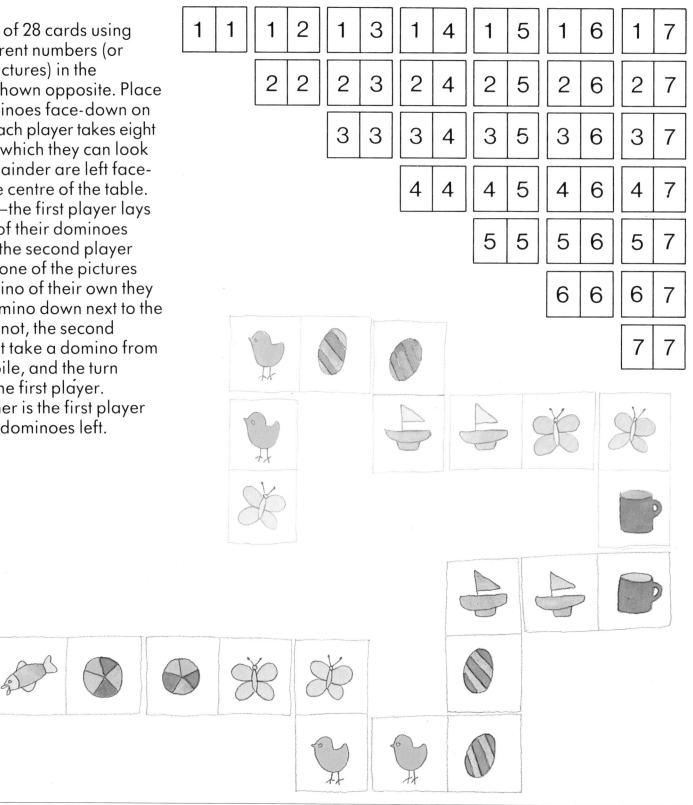

Numbers and counting

The meaning of numbers

Make use of everyday opportunities to help your child to understand the meaning of numbers and how they are used.

For example, when laying the table you could:

1 Talk about what 'one' represents, such as 'One knife for Mummy', 'One knife for Daddy', and so on.

2 Compare stacks of plates of different sizes.

3 Show how numbers of objects have nothing to do with size of objects. For example, is four of something always the same size? Try carrying in four teaspoons and then four chairs.

Counting

1 Count out piles of buttons, rice, raisins or similar objects into styrofoam trays or pots.

2 Make hand and foot prints (see page 18) and count the numbers of fingers and toes.

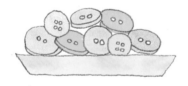

3 Make 'counting pictures', for example, lights on a Christmas tree, peas in a pod, a flock of birds, eggs in a nest, wheels on a train.

4 Draw different groups of objects on a large sheet of paper and put a circle around each group. Join the groups that have the same number of objects in them with a coloured line.

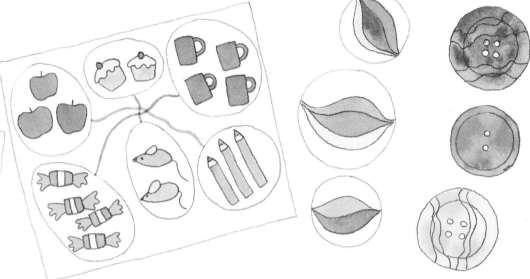

5 Place three buttons on a table. Ask your child to put three other objects next to them. Repeat this project with all the numbers that your child is learning.

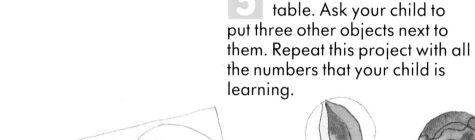

Picture Chart
Count all the people or vehicles passing your window during the space of, say, five or ten minutes. Draw a picture chart to show how many there were of each kind.

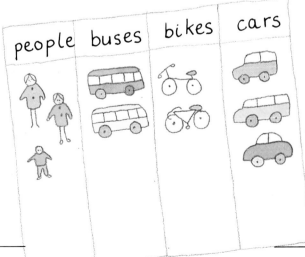

Jumping Jack

Make an articulated cardboard figure (see pages 132-133).

Draw a picture of a wide river with stepping stones across it. Make the puppet 'jump' from stone to stone and count the jumps.

Or, put some newspaper stepping stones on the floor so that your child can count their own jumps.

3 Draw the outlines of two groups of objects with a different number of objects in each group. Help your child to colour in, say, the larger group in red and the smaller in blue.

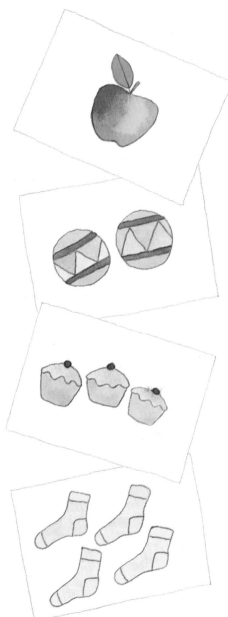

More or Less

Introduce the words 'more' and 'less'.

1 Place some buttons in a row of styrofoam trays in numerical sequence, i.e. one button in the first tray, two in the second, three in the third, etc.

By pointing to each tray from left to right, show how there is one more button in each tray. Then do the same thing but in the reverse sequence. (If you don't have enough buttons use nuts or pebbles or something similar.)

2 Make a selection of picture cards showing groups of objects from one to four. These can be arranged in various ways, showing cards going from low numbers to high, from high to low, or different groups of the same numbers.

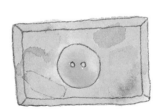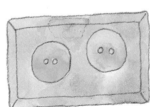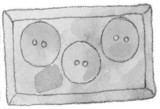

Number games

Number Dominoes

See page 102 for the sequence of designs and rules of play. Use dots to represent the numbers and only do the numbers from one to six. Make your cards more interesting by making a picture out of the dots, like the butterflies shown here.

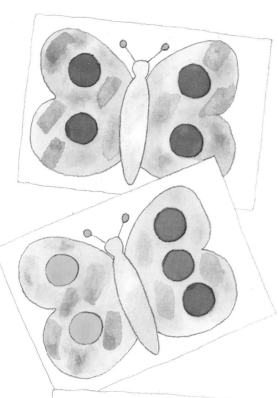
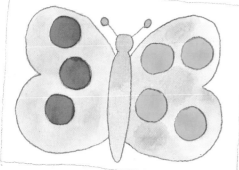

Jigsaw Game

Mount six pictures onto thick card, then divide each picture into six pieces. Clearly number each piece from one to six—using dots not figures. Make a dice (see page 109). For two players use two of the pictures, for three players use three pictures, and so on.

Show each player one completed jigsaw picture, then jumble up all the pieces and place them all face upwards in the middle of the table. The aim is for the players to collect the six pieces required to complete their picture.

To play—each player in turn shakes the dice and finds the piece from his or her picture that corresponds to the number shown on the dice. The winner is the first person to complete a picture.

Board games

Make some simple board games. They can represent either:

1 A single winding track, such as the route home from school, a treasure hunt, or a maze.

2 Parallel tracks, such as a race track or railway lines.

3 Adjacent squares, such as a 'snakes and ladders' game.

Keep the games fairly simple and try to work in jokes,

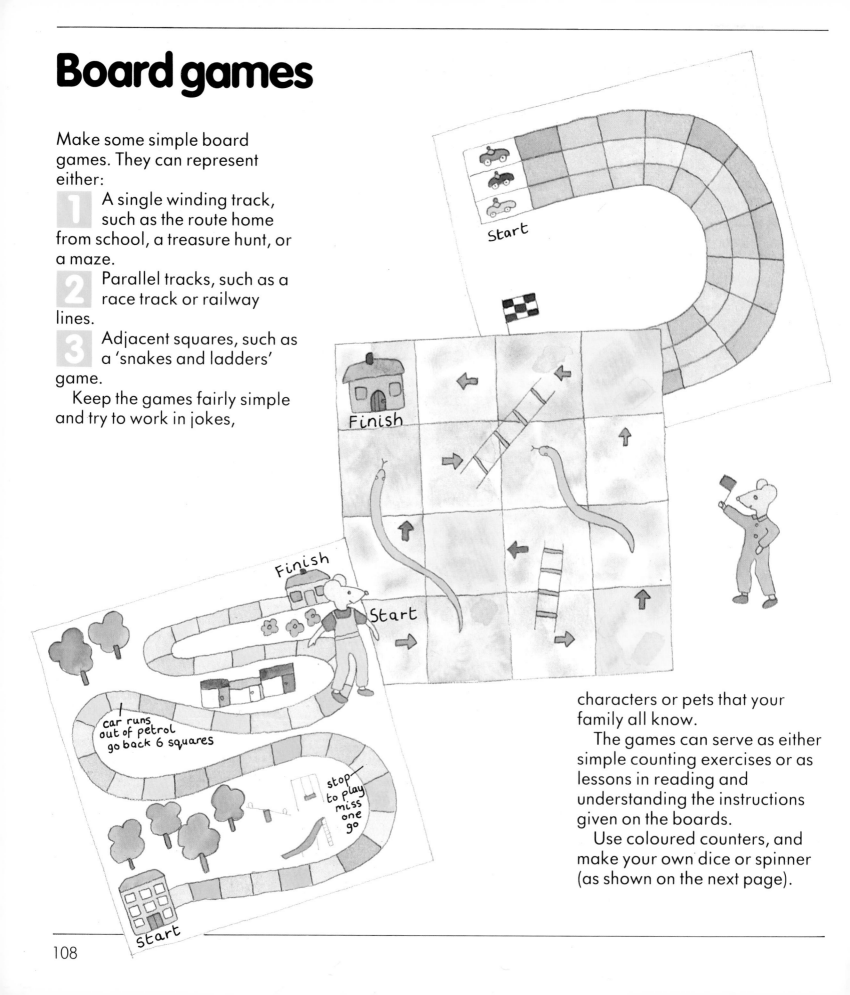

Start

Finish

Finish

Start

car runs out of petrol go back 6 squares

stop to play miss one go

Start

characters or pets that your family all know.

The games can serve as either simple counting exercises or as lessons in reading and understanding the instructions given on the boards.

Use coloured counters, and make your own dice or spinner (as shown on the next page).

Making dice and spinners

To Make a Dice

Trace around the diagram shown here. Cut out this shape from firm card and colour in the dots in the sequence shown.

Fold along all the dotted lines. Then glue the flaps to the sides with the matching letters—in alphabetical order—for example, flap 'a' to side 'a' and so on.

To Make a Spinner

Trace around the diagram shown here. Cut the hexagon shape from thick card. Draw on the lines and the numbers (or use dots instead of numbers). Push a cocktail stick or a pencil with a sharp point through the centre of the hexagon and spin it between thumb and forefinger.

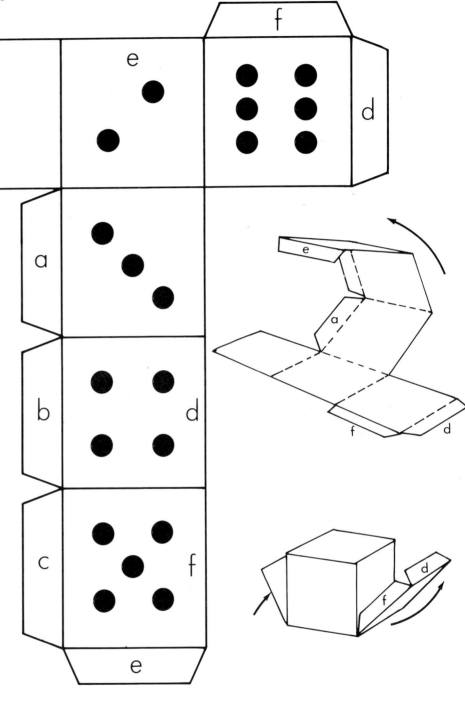

Number rhymes

The following number rhymes are just a few of the many that can be found in children's books. Where you can, act them out with your fingers while saying them.

You could also make up your own rhymes, for example:

> 1 2 3 4 Stephen's on the
>   kitchen floor,
> 5 6 7 8 counting biscuits on
>   his plate.

Or, using the tune of 'Ten Green Bottles' in other ways, for example:

> There are five shiny teaspoons
>   on the draining board,
> Five shiny teaspoons on the
>   draining board,
> And if one shiny teaspoon is
>   put into the drawer,
> There are four shiny teaspoons
>   on the draining board . . . .

And so on.

Buckle My Shoe
One, two, buckle my shoe,
Three, four, knock at the door,
Five, six, pick up sticks,
Seven, eight, shut the gate,
Nine, ten, a big fat hen.

(Traditional)

Who's Who?
Two legs sat upon three legs,
With one leg in his lap,
In comes four legs,
And runs away with one leg,
Up jumps two legs,
Catches up three legs,
Throws it after four legs,
And makes him bring back one leg.

(Traditional)

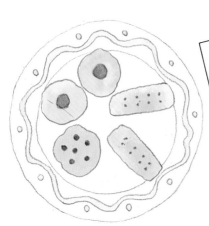

The Poor Widow
Here's to the poor widow from
  Babylon,
With six poor children all alone.
One can bake and one can brew,
One can shape and one can sew,
One can sit at the fire and spin,
One can bake a cake for the king.
Come choose you east, come choose
  you west,
Come choose the one that you
  love best.

(Traditional)

Ten Little Soldiers

Ten little soldiers
    Standing in a line,
One toddled home,
    And then there were nine.

Nine little soldiers
    Swinging on a gate,
One tumbled off,
    And then there were eight.

Eight little soldiers,
    Tried to fly to heaven,
One lost his wings,
    And then there were seven.

(and so on, through the next verses)
Seven . . . Playing silly tricks,
    One broke his neck,
Six . . . . . . Kicking all alive,
    One went to bed,
Five . . . . On a cellar door,
    One tumbled in,
Four . . . . Out on a spree,
    One got sick,
Three . . . Out in a canoe,
    One tumbled overboard,
Two . . . . Fooling with a gun,
    One shot the other,

One little soldier,
    With his little wife,
Lived in a castle,
    The rest of his life.

(Traditional)

How Many?

3 young rats with black felt
    hats,
3 young ducks with white straw
    hats,
3 young dogs with curling
    tails,
3 young cats with demi-veils,
Went out to walk with 2 young
    pigs,
In satin vests and sorrel wigs,
But suddenly it chanced to rain,
And so they all went home again.
(Traditional)

Recognizing and writing numbers

When your child seems to have a fairly clear idea of what numbers mean, you could help him or her to learn the symbols that represent the numbers.

Draw out the numbers your child knows in dotted lines so they can be traced over.

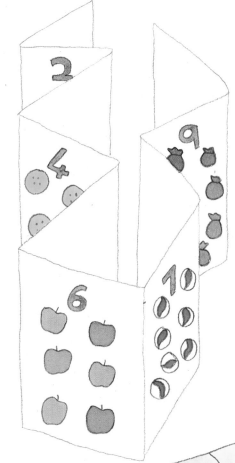

Number Jigsaws

Cut out ten cards. Write one of the numbers from one to ten on the top of each card and glue on or draw a group of simple objects of the same number below it.

Cut a wavy line between the number and picture on each card. Make sure the line is different for each one, to help your child match up the right picture with the right number.

Number Frieze

Fold up a long piece of paper, or stick a number of sheets together to make a frieze. Write the numbers from one to ten on the top of each sheet or folded section. Then stick pictures (or the objects themselves if they are light enough) underneath the numbers to illustrate each one.

Number Worm

Take a piece of thick card and draw a long wavy worm on it. Split the worm into ten segments and write the numbers from one to ten on each segment with the equivalent number of dots beside each number.

As you cut the segments up, make the curves of each cut different, so that the worm can only be reassembled with the numbers in the correct order.

Use practical examples to illustrate numbers to your child and, whenever possible, use real objects rather than pictures. For example:

Counting

1 'Let's do up your buttons—one, two, three . . .'

2 'How many people will be eating dinner?' . . . 'Here are all the knives and forks' . . . 'How many forks have you got . . . can you give everyone a fork?' . . . 'How many knives have you got . . . can you give everyone a knife?' . . . and so on, with spoons and dishes.

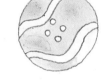

Adding On

1 'Here are two buttons . . . here are two more . . . how many are there now?'

2 'I have three pencils . . . pass me one more pencil . . . how many do I have now?'

Taking Away

1 'There are five biscuits on this plate. You eat one. How many are there now?'

2 'You have three dolls. If you give one doll to me, how many do you have left?'

Sharing

'Here are four cakes. How many people are there in the room? Will they each be able to have a cake?'

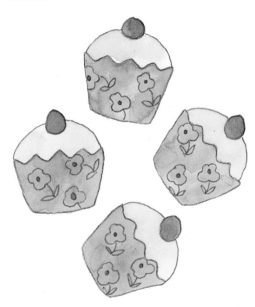

Shopping Games

You can buy and sell items around the house, such as toys, clothes or groceries, using buttons, counters or beans as money. Let one button represent one unit of money, such as one penny, so that there is no need to give change.

You could also collect a tin full of real pennies and play with them in the same way.

Measuring

Introduce these words wherever possible, and make some cards that you can ask questions about to help to illustrate their meaning: high—highest, low—lowest, big—biggest, small—smallest, many, most, less.

Who is the smallest?

Which monster has the most legs?

Which kite is flying the highest?

Which animal is the biggest?

Make a Simple Ruler

Cut out a strip of strong card about 3 cm by 20 cm and section off the card in 1 cm units along the ruler. (NB: Do not make your ruler in inches, as your child will be using the metric system in school.)

Use the ruler to measure books, doors, tables and other objects around the house.

| 1 | 2 | 3 | 4 | 5 | 6 | 7 | 8 | 9 | 10 | 11 | 12 | 13 | 14 | 15 | 16 | 17 | 18 | 19 | 20 |

Telling the time

Buy a simple clock face, or make one from strong card. Your clock should have moveable minute and hour hands—you can cut these from card also, and fix them to the centre of the clock with a metal paper fastener (split pin).

Move the hands around the clock to correspond with certain periods of the day, such as 'bed-time', 'getting-up', etc.

Set the times to the nearest hour at first, then introduce the half hour and, eventually, add the quarter hours, but do GO SLOWLY.

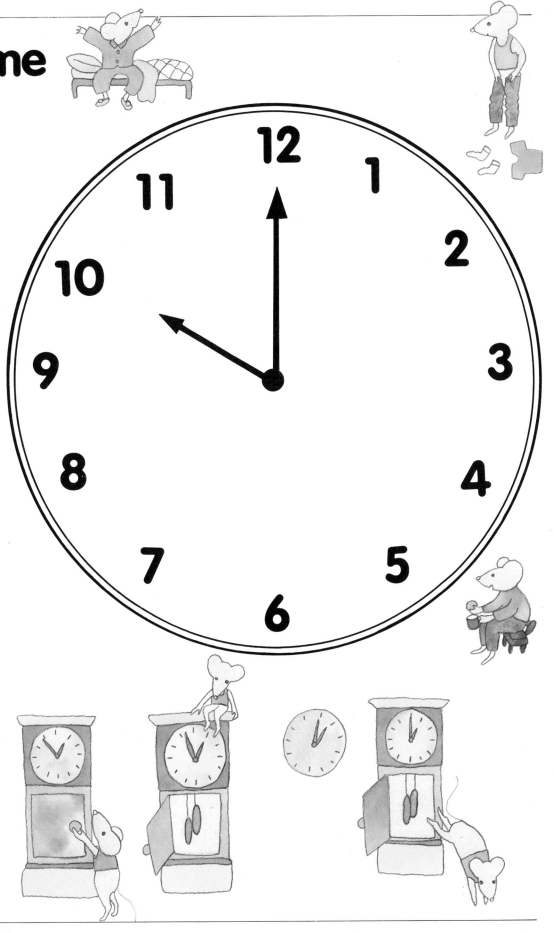

Tea-time for Timothy
Tell little Timothy
  it's nearly time for tea;
The ticker on the mantelpiece
  says half-past-three.
If he wants some tea today
  he'd better come and see.
There are strawberry tarts for Timothy
And buttered toast for me.
                    (Clive Sansom)

Hickory, Dickory, Dock
Hickory, Dickory, Dock,
A mouse ran up the clock,
The clock struck one,
The mouse ran down,
Hickory, Dickory, Dock.
                    (Traditional)

Today, tomorrow

Monday	
Tuesday	
Wednesday	
Thursday	
Friday	
Saturday	
Sunday	

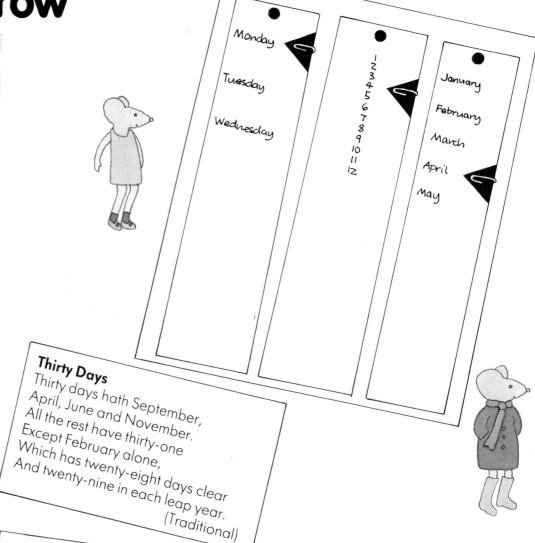

Today and Tomorrow
Does your child understand the following terms: day, night, morning, afternoon, evening, early, late, beginning, end, before, after, yesterday, today, tomorrow?

Sneeze on Monday
Sneeze on Monday,
Sneeze for danger.
Sneeze on Tuesday,
Kiss a stranger.
Sneeze on Wednesday,
Get a letter.
Sneeze on Thursday,
Something better.
Sneeze on Friday,
Sneeze for sorrow.
Sneeze on Saturday,
See your sweetheart tomorrow.
(Traditional)

Thirty Days
Thirty days hath September,
April, June and November.
All the rest have thirty-one
Except February alone,
Which has twenty-eight days clear
And twenty-nine in each leap year.
(Traditional)

Bed in Summer
In winter I get up at night
And dress by yellow candle-light.
In summer, quite the other way,
I have to go to bed by day.

I have to go to bed and see
The birds still hopping on the tree,
Or hear the grown-up people's feet
Still going past me in the street.

And does it not seem hard to you,
When all the sky is clear and blue,
And I should like so much to play,
To have to go to bed by day?
(Robert Louis Stevenson)

Make a calendar of the days of the week and illustrate it with pictures of activities that are familiar to your family.

You could also make a date calendar using three strips of card—the first strip listing the days of the week, the second the numbers from 1 to 31, the third the months of the year. Attach a marker to each strip—a triangle of coloured card held on by a paper clip will do. Position the marker against the relevant date each day.

Music and listening

Learning to listen

1 Hide a loudly ticking clock, or a transistor radio with the volume turned down, and see how quickly your child can find it.

2 Ask your child to close their eyes and listen to a sound that you will make, then try to guess correctly what the sound is. For example, you could shake a rattle; ring a bell; wind a clock or set off the alarm; jangle keys; tap fingers; rustle paper; close a door.

3 Both of you close your eyes and listen to sounds inside the room, or sounds you can hear outside. Talk about what you can hear and try to reproduce some of the sounds by voice and, later, by instruments.

4 Another day, both of you could try to reproduce sounds that your child knows well. For example, try the sound of footsteps; creaking or banging doors; a baby; the wind; a train; bees; a kettle whistling; a clock ticking; the telephone.

5 Talk about the different types of sounds. What happens to the noise made by a motor-bike as it approaches and goes away? Can you reproduce this sound?

Things That Go 'Bump'
Things that go 'bump' in the night,
Should not really give one a fright.
It's the hole in each ear
That lets in the fear,
That, and the absence of light!

(Spike Milligan)

Rhythm games

1 Let your child walk round in a circle while you clap, or beat out a drum rhythm. See if they can match their speed to yours. If your child is a bit self-conscious at first, it may help if you draw the circle on the floor, or outline it with a piece of tape.

2 Gradually increase the speed of the beat. Children will find this difficult at first because it involves careful listening, but when they can match the beat you can vary the game by introducing changes of direction.

3 Try beating out the rhythms of different sounds, like a soldier marching, a child running, or somebody walking.

4 Use a drum, rattle, bells or any kind of shaker to play a simple rhythm. Take up the rhythm with your body: stamp, tap your foot, nod to it, shake your legs and finally your whole body.

5 Hold conversations using rhythms—one of you taps out a simple rhythm (just three or four beats) and the other answers by repeating the message.

Loud and Soft

This may be a good time to introduce your child to the notion of 'loud' and 'soft'. Take a simple poem like 'Hot Cross Buns'. How loudly or softly can it be said? Try shouting the first two lines:

Hot cross buns!
Hot cross buns!

Whispering the next line:

One a penny, two a penny

And shouting the last:

Hot cross buns!

Or say the poem 'Follow-my-Leader' by Clive Sansom:

Follow-my-leader, follow-my-leader,
Follow-my-leader after me.
Follow me up to the top of the hill
And follow me down to the sea.

Let one person lead the others round the room. The leader recites the rhyme in as many different ways as they can, for example, loudly, softly, quickly, slowly, using similar movements to go with the sounds.

Extend the idea of loud and soft using a range of different noises, for example, shaking money or buttons in a tin, closing a door, crumpling newspaper. Make each noise twice, first as loudly as possible, then as quietly as possible.

Music and movement

Use the rhythms in well-known rhymes and songs to begin moving to sounds. Make sure that the rhythm suggests the type of movement as well as the words of the rhyme or song. Concentrate on one type of movement at a time. Dressing up may help—use floating chiffon scarves, full, flouncy skirts, flapping cloaks, and so on.

The rhymes and poems that follow will give you a few ideas.

Marching Rhymes

The Grand Old Duke of York

Oh the Grand Old Duke of York
He had ten-thousand men,
He marched them up to the top
 of the hill,
And he marched them down again.
And when they were up, they
 were up,
And when they were down, they
 were down,
And when they were only
 halfway up,
They were neither up nor down.

(Traditional)

Tum-Tumpty-Tum

Tum-tumpty-tum
The cat is banging the drum;
Four little mice are shaking
 the ground
Dancing merrily round and round,
Tum-tumpty-tum.

(Traditional)

(Repeat the above for the next three verses, but change the third line to 'three little mice', then 'two' then 'one'.)

Riding Rhymes

Ride-a-Cock Horse

Ride-a-cock horse to Banbury
 Cross,
To see a fine lady ride on a
 white horse.
With rings on her fingers,
And bells on her toes,
She shall have music wherever
 she goes.

(Traditional)

A Farmer Went Trotting

A farmer went trotting upon his
 grey mare,
Bumpety, bumpety, bump!
With his daughter behind him so
 rosy and fair,
Lumpety, lumpety, lump!
A raven cried, 'Croak!' and they
 all tumbled down,
Bumpety, bumpety, bump!
The mare broke her knees and
 the farmer his crown,
Lumpety, lumpety, lump!
The mischevious raven flew
 laughing away,
Bumpety, bumpety, bump!
And vowed he would serve them
 the same the next day,
Lumpety, lumpety, lump!

(Traditional)

Swinging Rhymes

The Clock Ticks
The clock
Ticks,
The clock
Tocks,
This way,
That way,
And never, never,
Stops.
Tick-tock
Tick-tock . . .

(Traditional)

Rowing Rhymes

Row, Row, Row the Boat
Row, row, row the boat
Gently down the stream
Merrily, merrily, merrily,
    merrily
Life is but a dream.

(Traditional)

Row, Boys Row
Row, boys row
As up the river we go
With a long pull
And a strong pull
Row, boys row.

(Traditional)

Rocking Rhymes

See-Saw Margery Daw
See-saw Margery Daw,
Johnny will have a new master,
He shall have but a penny a
    day,
Because he can't work any
    faster.

(Traditional)

Hush-a-Bye Baby
Hush-a-bye baby, on the tree
    top,
When the wind blows, the cradle
    will rock,
When the bough breaks, the cradle
    will fall,
Down will come baby, cradle and all.
(Traditional)

Swinging
Swing me low
Swing me high,
Over the grasses
As high as the sky.
Hair flying out,
Wind rushing by,
Like birds in the blue,
We sing as we fly,
Higher . . . .
Fly . . . .

(Traditional)

Spinning Rhymes

Ring-a-Ring of Roses

Ring-a-ring of roses,
A pocket full of posies,
A-tishoo, a-tishoo!
We all fall down.

(Traditional)

Wheels

Wheels, wheels, wheels,
Turning, turning, round and
    round
Wheels on buses, cars and
    trains
Faster, faster, they spin by
Round and round and round they
    fly.
Heavy wheels that turn machines,
Turning, pulling oh so slow.
Round and round and round they
    go.
Tiny wheels, inside a clock,
Whizz and whirr and jump and
    click
Round and round and round they
    tick.

(Anne Reay)

Tip-Toeing Rhymes

Tippy Tippy

Tippy tippy tippy tippy,
Tippy tippy tip-toe;
See the little hungry mice
Running in the snow, snow.

Tippy tippy tippy tippy,
Tippy tippy tip-toe;
They couldn't find a thing
    to eat
And so they had to go, go.

(Ruth Sansom)

Stamping Rhymes

As I Was Going

As I was going along, long,
    long,
A-singing a comical song, song,
    song,
The lane that I went was so
    long, long, long,
And the song that I sung was
    as long, long, long,
And so I went singing along.

(Traditional)

Upstairs Downstairs

Upstairs, downstairs,
Creeping like a mouse,
Creeping in the darkness
Round and round the house.
Creep, creep, creeping,
Round and round about –
I hope the wind won't come
    inside
And blow my candle out.

(Evelyn Abraham)

Hot Cross Buns

Hot cross buns!
Hot cross buns!
One a penny, two a penny
Hot cross buns!

(Traditional)

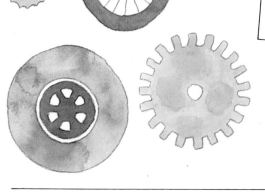

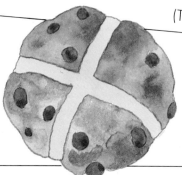

Making instruments

Make your child's first instruments from objects lying around the house. Use them to accompany any poems and songs you know.

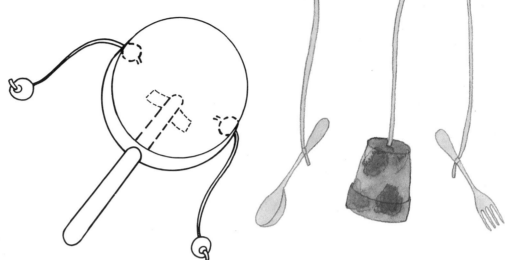

Percussion Instruments

1 Drums: Use upturned saucepans, plastic bowls, empty boxes or tins—cover the tops with greaseproof paper, or thick plastic, pulled tight and smooth and held in place by a thick elastic band.

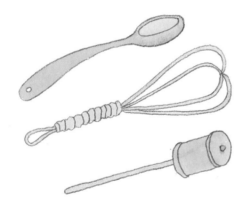

2 Drumsticks: Use spoons, cotton reels glued onto sticks, brushes, wire whisks.

3 Shakers: To introduce the idea, put some lentils, rice, pins or buttons into matchboxes. Then ask your child to guess which matchboxes contain which objects by shaking them. Experiment with different fillings and containers.

4 Japanese drums: Take a small, round empty food box (a wooden box makes the best sound). Push a stick through a hole in the side of the box and tape it to the inside of the bottom so that it acts as a handle. Make two more holes in the sides of the box and thread two pieces of string through the holes (with a knot on the inside to hold them). Fix a bead to the end of each string, and tape the lid on securely. Shake the box so that the beads bang against the sides.

5 Bells: Use a bunch of keys, or a string of foil bottle tops. Or thread some metal bottle tops onto a string and fasten them to a thick piece of wood (such as a piece of broom handle). Or, you could nail some individual tops loosely to the wood and bang the end on the ground so the tops ring.

6 Hanging bells: Hang anything metallic—nails, forks, foil dishes—or differently sized clay flowerpots from separate pieces of string. Tap them with a spoon or some other form of drumstick.

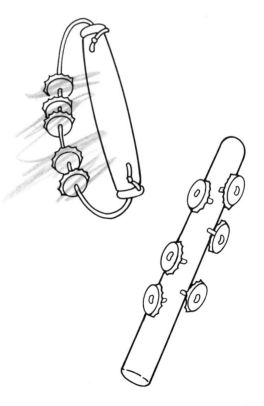

7 Cymbals: Use pairs of saucepan lids.

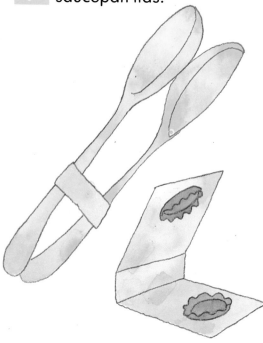

8 Castanets: Tape two spoons loosely together, as shown in the picture. Hold the handles firmly, and lightly tap out a rhythm on the palm of your free hand with the bowls of the spoon. Alternatively, take a strip of firm card about 4 cm by 20 cm (1½ ins by 8 ins), fold it in half and glue a metal bottle top to the inside of the two ends. With one hand, tap the bottle tops together.

Jingle Bells
Jingle bells, jingle bells,
Jingle all the way,
Oh what fun it is to ride,
In a one-horse open sleigh!
(Traditional)

9 Xylophone: Pour some water into a row of glasses or empty bottles, varying the level of the water in each one. Tap the sides lightly with a metal whisk and listen to the sound made by each. Experiment with the pitch by increasing and decreasing the water levels.

10 Woodblocks: Any two pieces of wood that can be banged or rubbed together will do. Stick a smaller piece of wood onto the back of each one as handles. For an interesting effect, cover one side of each block with sandpaper and scrape one block across the other. Compare the noises made by differently sized pieces of wood.

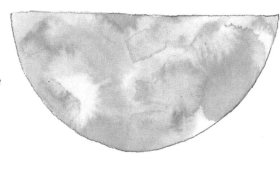

Wind Instruments

1 Trumpets: The simplest form of trumpet is a cardboard tube which you hum through, or a semi-circle of card rolled up to form a cone-shaped trumpet. Or, you could blow across the tops of empty plastic bottles.

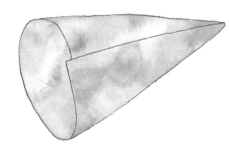

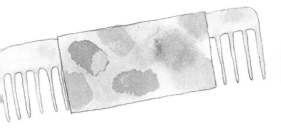

2 'Kazoo' comb: Fold a sheet of tissue paper over a large toothed comb. Press lips firmly against comb and tissue and hum.

Stringed Instruments

1 Double bass: Make two small holes (one at each end) in the bottom of a large, upturned cardboard box. Make six small cuts radiating out from one of the holes in the shape of a star. Push a broom handle through this hole and thread a piece of elastic through the other hole. Knot the end of the elastic inside the box and tie the other end to the top of the pole. Hold the pole firmly and pluck the elastic.

2 Zither: Stretch several elastic bands of different thicknesses around an open cardboard box and pluck. Make some small notches in the ends of the box to help to keep the elastic bands in place.

Alternatively, hammer a row of nails across one side of a rectangular piece of wood. Place another row of nails on the other side, directly opposite to the nails in the first row, but gradually decreasing the distance between the rows. Join each pair of nails with a taut elastic band and pluck.

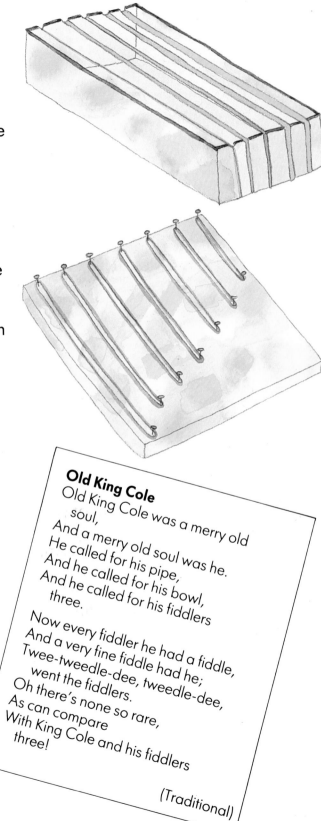

Old King Cole
Old King Cole was a merry old
soul,
And a merry old soul was he.
He called for his pipe,
And he called for his bowl,
And he called for his fiddlers
three.

Now every fiddler he had a fiddle,
And a very fine fiddle had he;
Twee-tweedle-dee, tweedle-dee,
went the fiddlers.
Oh there's none so rare,
As can compare
With King Cole and his fiddlers
three!

(Traditional)

Listening to music

A child's concentration is very limited. Begin by listening to short pieces, or tuneful movements from longer works. When introducing a piece of music, tap out some of the rhythms, or hum the main tunes, and talk about the mood of the music. Avoid imposing your own ideas on your child—music inspires different feelings in different people. Then, perhaps on another day, play the music again and discuss ways to move to the music, for example, run, skip, wriggle, slide, sway, crawl (nothing too complicated). Offer a wide choice of music to listen to.

Listening to Instruments
Examine pictures showing different instruments while listening to them on record or tape. Discuss the sounds made by the various instruments and compare their sizes and shapes with the variety of sounds they make.

Musical Statues
Choose a tape or record of lively dance music and begin dancing when the music is played. When it stops, the dancers have to 'freeze', like statues. Take a moment to look at the statues, then begin the music and dancing again.

All types of music can appeal to children, so encourage them to listen to a wide variety. For example, brass bands may inspire marching games, and both steel bands and pop music are good for dancing. To suggest individual records here would be impossible, as the pop charts are constantly changing, but listen out for songs with catchy rhythms and choruses.

Don't forget classical music, too. A list of suggestions is given below, but introduce your own favourites as well.

Britten – *Young Person's Guide to the Orchestra*
Debussy – *The Gollywog's Cake Walk*
Grieg – *Peer Gynt (The Dance of the Gnomes in the Hall of the Mountain King)*
Haydn – *Toy Symphony: Cello Concerto in D*
Holst – *The Planets*
Scott Joplin – *Piano Rags*
Kodaly – *Hary Janos Suite*
Mendelssohn – *Overture to A Midsummer Night's Dream*
Mozart – *Horn Concerto*
Rimsky-Korsakov – *The Flight of the Bumble Bee*
Saint-Saens – *The Carnival of the Animals*
Tchaikovsky – *The Nutcracker Suite*
Vivaldi – *The Four Seasons*

Play-acting

Finger and hand puppets

Puppets can be used to act out all kinds of simple rhymes and poems, and are a wonderful way of encouraging children to make up stories of their own.

The following examples show different ways of making simple finger and hand puppets.

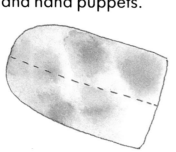

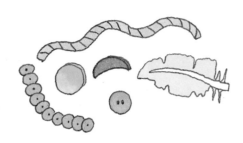

Five-Finger Rhyme
Dance thumbkin, dance,
Dance thumbkin, dance,
Dance ye merrymen every one,
But thumbkin he can dance alone,
Dance thumbkin, dance.

(Repeat for foreman, middleman, ringman and littleman.)

(Traditional)

Finger Puppets

1 Make a small animal, using a scrap of felt or fur folded in half and stitched up the side. Stitch on a piece of string for the tail and bits of felt for the ears.

2 Cut the fingers from an old glove. Glue on eyes, nose, mouth, etc, using felt or paper scraps, feathers, buttons and beads.

3 Draw a picture on firm cardboard, then cut it out. Make a ring of paper to fit the top of your finger and glue or sellotape it onto the back of the picture. You could cut out simple animal shapes or figures, then colour them in and glue on scraps of material to decorate them.

4 Knit a puppet: Use double-knit wool and size 10 needles.
Cast on 20 stitches.
Knit 26 rows.
Knit two together along the 27th row.
Cut the wool, leaving a loose end of about 20 cm (8 ins), and sew the end of the wool back

through the stitches. Slide the stitches off the needle and pull the end of the wool to gather them tightly together. Oversew the end to secure it. Sew the two edges together. Stuff the top with pieces of stocking or cotton wool to make a head, and gather the puppet tightly under the stuffing to make a neck. Make a face and some hair, using buttons and scraps of wool.

5 Cut out a cardboard figure about 12 cm (5 ins) tall, without legs. Make two holes in the base of the trunk. Put your second and third fingers through the holes to give the puppet legs.

Hand Puppets

1 Use the palm of your hand. Simply draw on a face then wriggle your fingers and thumb and watch the face move.

2 Draw a face on a small paper bag. Tie up the two corners to represent ears. Or fold down the top of the bag to make a mouth that moves.

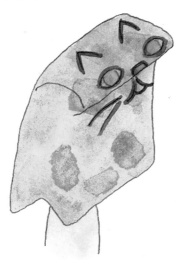

Five Little Ducks

Five little ducks went out to
   play,
Over the hills and far away.
Mother Duck said, 'Quack, quack,
   quack',
And only four little ducks came
   back.

(Repeat for four ducks, then three, then two, then one, then the final verse:)

Mother Duck went out one day,
Over the hills and far away.
Mother Duck said, 'Quack, quack,
   quack',
And five little ducks came
   swimming back.

(Traditional)

3 Take an old wooden spoon and paint a face on the back of the spoon bowl. Tie material round the neck to hide the handle.

4 Paint a face on the top half of a cardboard tube, and stick scraps of wool or fur on it for hair. Glue some material around the bottom half to hide your hand.

5 Make two rolls of paper, one longer and thinner than the other. Twist the thin roll around the larger one to make arms on a body, and fasten with sellotape. Decorate the puppet with a face and hair.

6 Take an old sock and push in the toe end to make a mouth. Put a few stitches in each side of the mouth to hold the shape. Sew on buttons for the eyes, and a piece of felt to make a tongue. To alter the shape of the head, put some stuffing inside it.

The Serpent
The serpent with his slender slimness slithers slowly southwards.
His slimy cotton-stitched back slides behind him.
He stops,
Pauses
Now he slides off into shadowy silence.

(David Mathys)

7 Fold a paper plate in half and glue some material to the plate about 2 cm (¾ in) above the fold. Use the material to hide your hand.

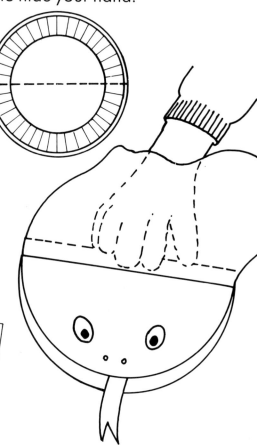

8 Put a yoghurt pot or plastic cup inside the toe of a stocking to make a head. Glue or sew on scraps to decorate the face.

Decorations
Use paint; string; wool; raffia; strings of beads; fur; buttons; foil bottle tops; scraps of material, and anything else you can think of.

String and stick puppets

Spiders

Thread eight pieces of string with foil bottle tops (knot the string as you go, to hold the tops in place). Punch eight holes into the lid of a margarine tub and thread one end of each string through a hole and knot it.

Make a hole in the bottom of the tub. Loop and knot some more string and thread it through the tub bottom to make a hanger. Paint the tub with thick paint mixed with some paste, or stick paper around it and draw on eyes and a mouth.

Little Miss Muffet
Little Miss Muffet,
Sat on a tuffet,
Eating her curds and whey.
Along came a spider,
Which sat down beside her,
And frightened Miss Muffet away.
(Traditional)

Ghosts

Tie enough net, nylon or silk pieces to the neck of a balloon so that it covers the balloon completely. Stick large paper eyes and a mouth onto the material, and let the 'ghost' float from a string tied round the neck and fixed to the ceiling.

Snakes

Thread some yoghurt pots onto a length of string—knot the string as you go to hold the pots in position. Find some thin sticks (like the ones that are used to support garden plants) and sellotape the end of one stick to the head of the snake, and the other stick to the end part of the body. If you make a very long snake use four sticks, so that two people can move the snake together.

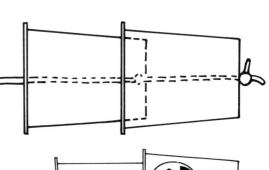

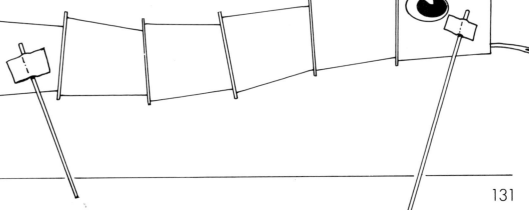

Hinged and shadow puppets

Hinged Puppets
Practise making hinged puppets by cutting out a variety of shapes from stiff card and joining them together with split pins so that the various parts can be moved.

Dragons
Cut a dragon's body out of stiff card in three separate pieces—the head, the body and the tail. Join the pieces together using metal paper fasteners (split pins) so that the separate pieces each have a certain amount of movement. Tape one stick to the head part and one to the tail part.

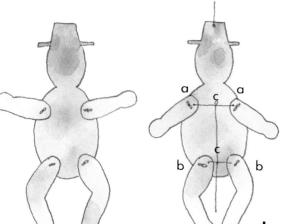

Jumping Jack
Cut out one piece of card in the shape of a body and head, then cut out two arms and two legs. Fasten the arms and legs to the body with split pins so they can move freely.

Using three pieces of strong thread (one long piece and two short pieces):
a) make two small holes in the top of the arms and thread one short piece of string through the holes to join them together;
b) make two holes in the top of the legs and use the other short piece of string to join these together;

c) tie the long piece of string to the middle of the two short pieces leaving about 15 cm (6 ins) hanging below the body.

Make a hole in the top of the head and reinforce it with sellotape. Thread another piece of string through the hole. Hang the puppet up by this piece of string. Pull the hanging thread (c) to make the puppet jump.

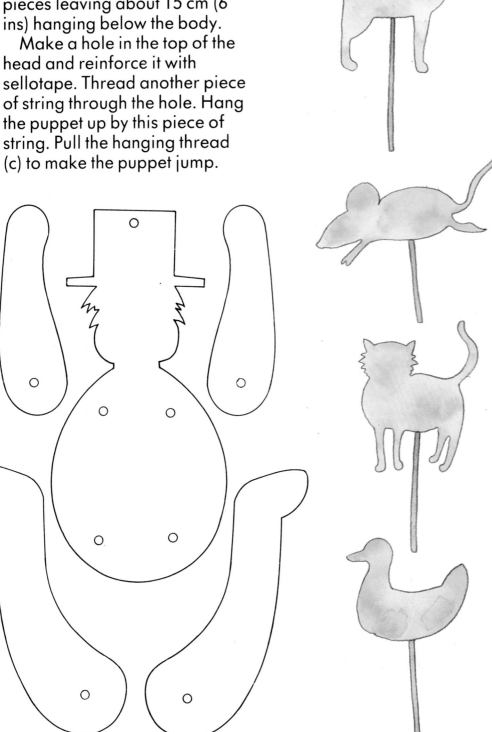

Shadow Puppets

Cut out silhouettes of animals or figures from stiff card and tape a stick to each one. To make groups of animals (for example, three mice) stick the silhouettes onto a strip of strong card to form a base, then tape a stick to the base. Choose characters from favourite rhymes or stories.

Make a translucent screen. For example, hang a sheet of white cotton or a large piece of greaseproof paper across part of an open doorway or down the side of a table. Fix the screen so that it is as smooth and firmly held as possible. Use a table lamp or desk lamp to shine a light on the back of the screen and close the curtains to darken the rest of the room.

The puppet player stands on the same side as the light and holds up the puppets against the screen. The audience sits on the other side of the screen so that they see the puppets through the screen.

Making masks

Always make large eye-holes in masks so your child can see clearly. The eye-holes can be in addition to the eyes for the mask face if you want to decorate the eyes for the face.

1 Cut the back and the opened end off a cereal box and make a hole in each side of the box. Thread some elastic through the holes to hold the mask in place. Paint over the box or cover it with plain paper, then decorate it with scraps of material or paper. Cut out the eye holes, and a flap for the nose if you wish.

2 Decorate a paper bag; cut holes for the eyes and tie up the corners to make ears. If the bag is a long one, cut up the sides a little so that it will fit over your child's shoulders.

3 Decorate a paper plate and either thread elastic through it to hold it in place, or tape it onto a stick so that the stick makes a handle to hold the mask in front of the face.

4 Make a papier-mâché mask, like the one shown on page 31.

5 Use the shape shown in the illustration below as a guide, and cut out a similar shape from stiff card. Make it large enough to fit round your child's head. Mark out the shape of the eyes lightly in pencil and then cut them out. Bend the straps a, b and c into position and then adjust them to fit the head. Glue the straps into position. Make a paper cone for a nose, and glue on some ears, or a cone hat and wool or string hair.

Dressing up

Collect a box of odd bits of clothing and pieces of material. Particularly useful are things that can be used in several ways, such as skirts, shoes, scarves, shawls, shirts, hats, ties. Also objects that suggest particular characteristics or occupations, such as glasses (without lenses), eyeshades, uniforms, bags, a tool box, and so on.

Dressing-Up Games

1 Pick-a-person: Scatter the clothes round the room. One person stands in the middle of the room and another person gives directions, for example, 'Walk forward', 'Turn to the door', 'Take two steps', 'Stop'. At the word 'Stop' the person being directed picks up the nearest item of clothing and puts it on. Repeat this until they have picked up about four pieces of clothing, then look in a mirror (a full-length mirror is best). Talk about who the person might be who would dress like that. Make up a name for the character or a few words that would describe them.

2 Suitcase game: Put a pile of old clothes and props on the floor and put an empty cardboard box alongside them. One person picks up an article, for example, a red hat, and puts it in the box saying, 'I'm going on holiday and I will take . . . . my red hat'. The next person also puts something in the box, for example, a blue shirt, and says 'I'm going on holiday and I'll take . . . my red hat and blue shirt'.

Continue the game, increasing the list of things in the box until one person forgets something.

3 'And a-this-a-way': Think of some characters you all know well, such as those from nursery rhymes, favourite stories, or television characters. One person thinks of a character and dresses up to look like them. Then they move around in the way that the character would, saying:

When I was a lady (gentleman/ king/little boy, or whatever) And a . . . . was I, A-this-a-way and a-this-a-way And a-this-a-way went I.'

4 Clothes shop: Sort the clothes into different 'departments'—hats, shoes, coats, and so on. Buy and sell them, introducing words such as too small, larger, thick, thin, short, heavy, light and dark.

Acting games

Lots of nursery rhymes and poems are fun to act out. Here are a few ideas, but you and your child will probably have lots more favourites of your own.

Going to the Sea
Walk:
Walking in my red shoes,
Down the busy street,
Walking in my red shoes,
Whom do you think we'll
     meet?
"Hullo Jane."
Tramp:
Tramping in my black
     shoes,
Down the muddy lane,
Tramping in my black
     shoes
Through the dripping rain.
Skip:
Skipping on my bare toes,
Beside the sandy sea,
Up the beach and back again,
Up the beach and back again
And into the rolling sea.
Swim:
I swim – and I swim,
On the billows – I ride,
I float – and I float
With the swing of the
     tide.
Skip:
Then out of the sea,
And on to the sand,
I skippety-skip
To the beat of the band
And away from the rolling
     sea.
(Ruth Sansom)

Elephant Walk
Plonk on this foot,
Plonk on that,
Swinging my trunk,
Swinging my trunk.
I'm out in the jungle
Without any hat,
Plonk on this,
Plonk on that!
I'll go to sleep
In the shade of a tree,
Nose on knee,
Nose on knee,
And no one will know
That it's only me,
Nod and nod,
Sleep and sleep.
(Ruth Sansom)

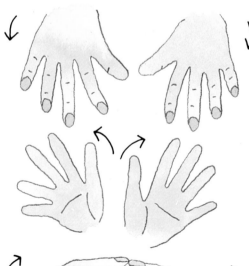

Incy Wincy Spider
(Use hand movements only for this, as shown in the diagrams opposite.)
Verse 1:
Incy Wincy Spider
Climbed the water spout,
Verse 2:
Down came the rain
And washed poor Incy
     out.
Verse 3:
Out came the sun and
Dried up all the rain
Verse 4:
Incy Wincy Spider
Climbed up the spout
     again.
(Traditional)

Simon Says

One person leads, saying, 'Simon says do this' and at the same time making a simple movement. The other person imitates the action. As your child improves at the game, make it a little harder by occasionally omitting the words 'Simon says' and just saying 'Do this'. When this happens the other player must not copy the action. If they do, they will be 'out' and they become the leader.

Shadows

Hang up an old sheet, or clear a space on a white wall, to act as a 'screen'. Shine a light onto your screen and put your hands, or your whole body, in front of the light to cast a shadow. See how many shadow shapes you can make. For example, you can use your hands to make a bird or a rabbit's head with floppy ears, and use your body to make a gorilla or a monster.

Telephones

Make your own telephone by joining two yoghurt pots with a piece of string. Bore a hole in the bottom of the pots, thread one end of the string through each pot and knot it. Pull the pots apart so that the string is taut. One person speaks into one pot, while the other person listens through the other pot.

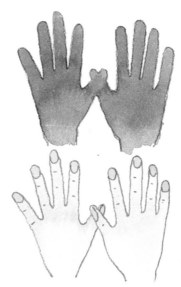

Hands

Hands are very handy things,
Hands can wash things,
Hands can squash things,
Hands can gently pat your head.
Hands can clap,
Hands can flap,
Hands can point like this or that.
Hands can make things,
Hands can shake things,
Hands can flutter, just like wings.
Hands can fold,
Hands can hold,
Hands are very handy things.

(Ogden Nash)

Today I Feel . . .

Using props and costumes to help, take turns to act out a mood. For example, anger, excitement, fear, happiness. You could turn this into a guessing game, but don't be too rigid—allow answers that are nearly right.

Jelly Game

Collect (or draw) pictures of things that move in different ways, for example, jelly on a plate, a rag doll, an elastic band, a balloon, a tumble drier, clothes on a washing line, a wave in the sea, and so on. Mount the pictures onto cards, then put the cards face down in a stack. Each player picks up a card in turn and acts out the movements of the object in the picture. The other players try to guess what the object is.

The game can also be played using animal cards (some animal shapes are given on pages 147-148). With animals. the players can make noises as they move.

Make Believe

Act out recent experiences, such as a visit to the shops, a bus or train ride, the hairdresser's, the doctor's, or mending the car. Or, act out imaginary things, like being an astronaut, exploring caves or tunnels, or camping.

Suggest a few props or costumes to help, but encourage the children to think up their own ideas as well—they may not think that the wastepaper bin makes a good space helmet, even if you do!

Jelly
Jelly on the plate,
Jelly on the plate,
Wibble, wobble, wibble, wobble,
Jelly on the plate.

(Traditional)

Aa Bb Cc Dd Ee

7

Word-building and story-telling

Using words

Shopping Lists

Build up a list of words (this trains the memory, too). One person begins by saying, 'I went to the shops and bought . . .', then naming one item. The next person repeats the sentence including the item and adds a purchase of their own. The game continues until someone forgets the list.

To play the game with younger children—put a variety of objects out on the table. As they are named, the objects are picked up and moved to the front of the table.

The same game can be played with a different introductory line, for example, 'In the zoo there were . . . . elephants' and so on.

Feelies

Hide some toys or other objects in paper bags. Ask your child to put a hand into each bag in turn and guess what is inside without looking. Ask them to describe each object as they feel it, for example, 'It is hard . . . cold . . . rough . . . smooth . . . round . . . hollow . . . solid . . . curved . . . crooked'. . . and so on.

Similes

How many words can you think of to fill these gaps?

As quiet as . . . . . .
As loud as . . . . . .
As hard as . . . . . .
As small as . . . . . .

Change the sentences to be appropriate to whatever you are doing at the time.

Riddles

Invent some 'What am I' riddles. For example:

1. Riddle me! riddle me!
   What is that
   Over your head and under your hat?
(Answer: hair)

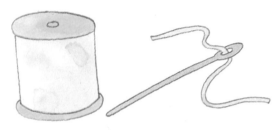

2. With my little eye,
   Nought can I spy,
   But, BEWARE
   A sharp point have I.
(Answer: needle)

3. It scratches and tugs
   And hurt it might,
   But its sharp teeth
   Can never bite
(Answer: comb)

Tongue Twisters
There is a good collection of tongue twisters in the book *Talking Rhymes* published by Ladybird. See if you can invent some of your own. Here are a few just to start you off:

1. Moses supposes his toeses
   are roses,
   But Moses supposes
   erroneously;
   For nobody's toeses are
   posies of roses
   As Moses supposes his toeses
   to be.
2. Billy Button bought a buttered
   biscuit.
   Did Billy Button buy a
   buttered biscuit?
   If Billy Button bought a
   buttered biscuit,
   Where's the buttered biscuit
   that Billy Button bought?
3. She sells sea-shells on the
   sea-shore.

Playing with Words
As you sing or say familiar nursery rhymes, try putting in the wrong word for your listeners to spot the mistake. For example:
   Baa Baa Black *cow* (sheep)
   Have you any wool?
   Yes sir, yes sir,
   Three bags *sausages* (full)
   One for the master
   One for the *kangaroo* (dame)
   And one for the little boy
      who lives down the lane.
Or leave out the second of two rhyming words for someone else to fill in the gap:
   Little Polly Flinders,
   Sat among the . . . .
      (cinders)
   Warming her pretty little toes.
   Her mother came and caught
      her,
   And whipped her little
      . . . . (daughter)
   For spoiling her nice new
      clothes.

Illustrating Words
Draw some words on a large sheet of paper and decorate them to give a clue to their meaning.

Question and Answer Poems

Make up rhyming words to answer questions—the words can be nonsensical, as long as they rhyme. For example:

What's your name?
Sarah Jane.
Where do you live?
In a sieve.
What's your number?
Cucumber.
What's your town?
Upside down.

Rat-a-Tat Tat

Rat-a-tat tat
Who is that?
Only grandma's pussycat.
What do you want?
A pint of milk.
Where is your money?
In my pocket.
Where is your pocket?
I forgot it.
Oh you silly pussycat!

(Traditional)

Moving to Words

Think of some words that are fun to say: hiss, hoop, tiptoe, pop, buzz, giggle, showery, drippy, zoo, slide, oblong, slipper, wobble, and so on.

Invent movements (flicking fingers, flapping, stabbing, winding, curling, stretching) to accompany some of the words—move around the room repeating them. Experiment with the way you say the words (whispering, shouting, singing). Try using instruments that match the sounds of the words as you say them (see pages 123-125).

Sound Words

Make up words to match familiar sounds and noises, like the sound of a vacuum cleaner, or rain falling, or people walking in wellington boots or soft slippers.

In the Rain

Swishing, swashing down the lane,
Come the lorries in the rain.
Shunkle, shonkle is the mutter,
Of water flowing down the gutter.
Shillop, shallop through the mud,
Go the cows chewing the cud.
Splashing, splishing, cars go by,
But I'm inside and nice and dry!

(Daphne Lister)

Action poems

Try saying the following poems and make the actions to go with them. In the first poem, the first two verses represent a train approaching the brow of a hill, in the last verse the train races down the hill.

Eletelephony

Once there was an elephant
Who tried to use the telephant—
No! No! I mean an elephone
Who tried to use the telephone—
(Dear me! I am not certain quite
That even now I've got it right.)

Howe're it was, he got his trunk
Entangled in the telephunk,
The more he tried to get it free,
The louder buzzed the telephee—
(I fear I'd better drop the song
of elephop and telephong!)

(Laura E. Richards)

The Airman

rrrrrrrrrrrrr

The engine roars,
The propeller spins,
"Close the doors!"
Our flight begins.

zzzzzzzzzzzzz

The plane rises;
It skims the trees.
Over the houses
We fly at our ease.

mmmmmm

ZOOM goes the plane,
The engine hums.
Then home again,
And down it comes . . . . .

(Clive Sansom)

The Steam Train and the Hill

wish I could
   I wish I could
      I wish I could

I think I can
   I think I can
      I think I can.

I thought I could,
   I thought I could,
      I thought I could . . . . .

(Clive Sansom)

These poems are from an anthology by Clive Sansom called *Speech Rhymes*, published by A & C Black Ltd. If you enjoy words and their sounds, you'll like this book of poems.

Scrapbooks

Cut some sheets of thick plain or coloured paper (sugar paper) to about 25 cm by 40 cm (10 ins by 16 ins) and fold them in half. Either staple along the fold to hold the sheets together (although this can make them hard to open out) or sew down the fold. Keep your first scrapbooks short (about four pages only). Write your child's name in clear letters on the front so that he or she feels the importance of having their own book. (The best way to form letters for young children is shown opposite.)

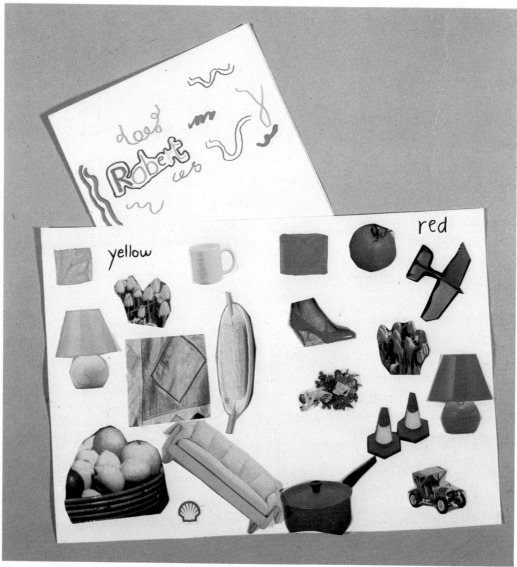

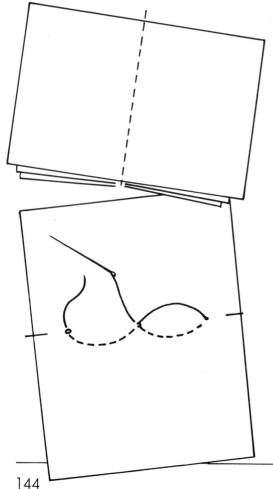

Topics

1 A collection of pictures (cut from magazines)—encourage your child to group them according to their subject. For example, a page for food, clothes, flowers, and so on.

2 Colours—if your child has just learnt to distinguish colours, why not make a book with one page for each colour? Put a dab of the particular colour at the top of the page and write the name of the colour alongside; underneath, stick pictures from magazines and your child's own drawings in the same colour.

3 Me—include some photographs and/or your child's own drawings of their family, house, toys and pets. Write the names of each in a simple sentence underneath.

Shaping letters

When writing for your children, on their paintings or books, be particularly careful about forming your letters clearly. Always use letters in lower-case (i.e. 'small' letters), except when a capital letter is necessary, such as for the first letter of a proper name—Mark, Lisa.

The letters shown on this page are an example of a good style to follow. I have also included arrows to show how the letters should be formed. When your children are taught to write, they will use a similar method to this. For more information on teaching children to write see the next chapter.

Making friezes

Friezes are a colourful way to tell a story. Build a scene by pasting cuttings from magazines or paintings onto a large sheet of paper, or draw pictures on the paper yourself. Use a piece of plain lining paper (from a wallpaper shop), or the back of a remnant of old wallpaper. Then tell a story to go with the pictures.

Make the pictures large and colourful and don't try to put in too much detail. Choose a subject that your child is interested in at the time, such as a Christmas scene, a circus, a space adventure, a frightening forest, or a birthday party (if you draw in the figures yourself your child could colour them in to look like friends or family).

Friezes can also illustrate nursery rhymes or songs, for example, 'The animals went in two by two' (Noah's Ark); 'Old Macdonald had a farm'; 'There was an old woman who swallowed a fly'.

On the following pages, you will see some outlines of animals to help you draw them yourself. As you can see, it is possible to keep the shapes simple and yet still be able to recognize them.

Animal shapes

1. The animals went in two by two,
   Hurrah, Hurrah!
   The animals went in two by two,
   Hurrah, Hurrah!
   The animals went in two by two,
   The elephant danced with the
     kangaroo,
   And they all went in to the
     ark, for to get out of the
     rain.

2. The animals went in three by
     three, Hurrah, Hurrah!
   The animals went in three by
     three, Hurrah, Hurrah!
   The animals went in three by
     three,
   The wolf was stung by the
     bumble bee,
   And they all went in to the
     ark, for to get out of the
     rain.

3. The animals went in four by
     four, ...
   The great hippopotamus stuck
     in the door,

4. The animals went in five by
     five, ...
   The snail ran in to stay alive,

5. The animals went in six by
     six, ...
   On the back of the turtle the
     monkey did sit,

6. The animals went in seven by
     seven, ...
   The little pig thought he was
     going to heaven,

7. The animals went in eight by
     eight, ...
   The snake rode on the zebra,
     because he was late,

continued . . .

8. The animals went in nine by
      nine, ...
   The frog jumped in at the end
      of the line,

9. The animals went in ten by
      ten, ...
   If you want any more you must
      sing it again.

(Adapted)

Picture stories

Start a collection of cards and magazine cuttings, then give your child some empty chocolate or shoe boxes and get them to divide the pictures into subjects, for example, views and people. Stick a picture onto the lid of each box to indicate what subject is inside.

The pictures can be used to encourage speech and conversation:

1 Ask your child questions about a picture—'Who are the people?', 'What are they doing?' Try to encourage closer observation by discussing clothes, the weather, the season, and so on. If this provokes no response, try another picture.

2 Draw a face onto the back of your (or your child's) hand so that the fore and middle fingers become 'legs'. Or, use the puppet shown on page 129. Lay four postcards with contrasting views face upwards on the table. 'Walk' your hand across each scene in turn and describe where you are and what you see.

3 Select some pictures and lay them out on the table. Then build up a story by briefly describing each picture.
A more difficult version of this game is to take six picture cards, shuffle them and then place them face down on the table. Turn over one card at a time and invent a story by saying a sentence about each picture. Keep your sentences very simple.

Story ideas

(For telling, not reading)

1 For first stories, look for simple ideas:
A walk in the park
A visit to a shop
A day by the sea

2 Make up stories about the people you see visiting the street outside your house, such as the milkman, postman, paper boy or girl, window cleaner. Take each person in turn and describe what happens as they visit three or four houses. Is anyone at home? Is a note left? How many pints of milk/letters are delivered? Does the paper boy whistle loudly?

Children enjoy stories with repetition as they can guess what's going to happen, so introduce repetition into your stories—at the fourth house a dog always barks and scares the visitor away, so they are left with no letters, milk or papers, and have dirty windows.

3 The train journey: Draw a railway track across a blackboard or sheet of paper. Then move a cardboard or toy train along the track, describing what the passengers see. As you talk, paste on pictures or draw simple stick people and animals to illustrate the story.

A walk around the town (farm, zoo, park or whatever) can be told in the same way.

4 'It has to be something special': Draw a plan of the shops in a shopping centre. Sarah is moving from shop to shop, looking for a birthday present for her mother, and food for a birthday tea. Invent a conversation that can be repeated in every shop (perhaps using the words in the title); eventually she finds the right present.

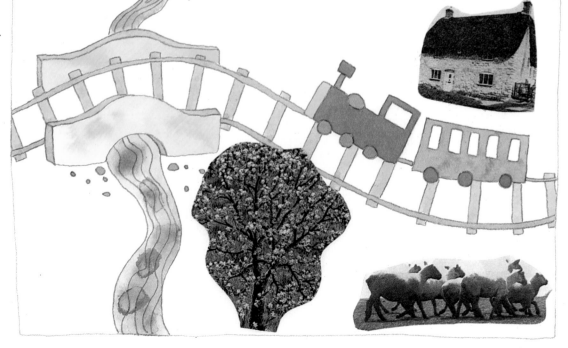

5 'Where do I live?': Draw a simple picture to illustrate the story given below. Give your child a duck made of cardboard or plastic to move across the picture as the duck in the story waddles round the farm.

The Story
A duckling leaves his nest and goes for a walk.

Tired and lonely, he realizes he has forgotten where he lives. He sees a hole in the ground, looks in and asks 'Is this where I live?'

'No!' – out jumps a fox and says, 'This is my home.' And frightens the duckling away.

Repeat the same formula with the duck looking into a tree at a bird's nest; finding a mouse's nest amongst the corn; a chicken's nest in the barn; finally, a boy in the farmhouse. The boy then picks up the duckling and takes him to the pond where his mother is waiting.

As an alternative: draw the picture on a blackboard, putting in each piece as you tell the story.

Other ways to illustrate stories

1 Tell a story leaving out some of the words and holding up pictures that represent the words instead, so that your child can guess what the words are.

2 Put a few household objects on the table and make up a story around them. Your child can pick up the appropriate objects at certain stages of the story.

3 Felt boards: For shorter stories with few characters. Cover a piece of thick card about 20 cm by 30 cm (8 ins by 12 ins) with felt and secure it firmly so that it is very tight and smooth with no creases. Cut out cardboard pictures of the characters in a story (and one or two major objects if necessary, such as a house). Glue some pieces of felt onto the back of the cardboard characters so that they stick to the felt board.

As you tell the story, display the characters and objects on the board. Story suggestions:

Goldilocks and the Three Bears
The Ugly Duckling
The Three Little Pigs
Little Red Riding Hood
Jack and Jill

4 Photographs: Tell your child something about your own childhood, using photographs as illustrations. Where did your parents live? Who are your brothers and sisters? Do they have any children now? What did you do as a child at Christmas or on a family outing?

5 Using toys: Use toys to act out some stories. For example, a doll and teddy bears would be an obvious choice for 'Goldilocks and the Three Bears'. By making simple props and costumes (crowns, cloaks, helmets), the toys can be used to play many characters.

Preparing to read and write

Getting started

The best way to prepare children for reading is by showing them a good example. Share your enjoyment of books with them and read to them regularly. Join the children's section of your local library. If you have any adult reference books with colourful and interesting illustrations in them, show these to your child as well.

I have not attempted to describe the teaching of reading and writing in detail here, as this has already been thoroughly covered by an excellent book called *Reading Through Play* by Carol Baker, published by Macdonald Educational Ltd. However, in this chapter you will find some additional ideas for games to help your child develop these vital skills.

Pencil Control

Remember that pencil control does not come easily to most children so never try to force it. Use large crayons to begin with and let your child cover the paper with dots, dashes, a continuous winding line, or crosses.

1 Draw any of the patterns shown here for your child to trace over with a crayon. Or use any simple patterns you can think of.

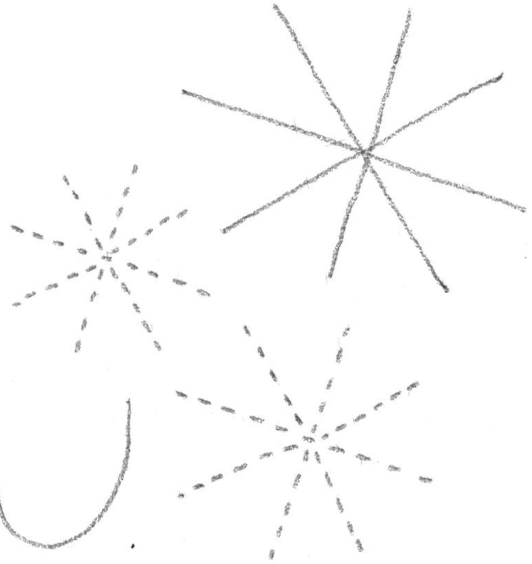

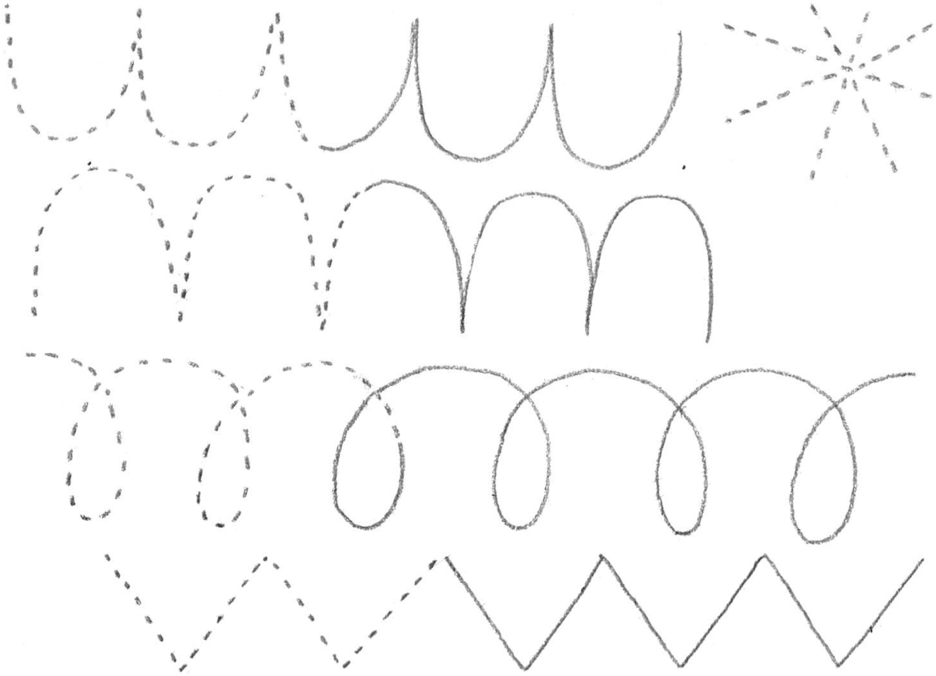

2 Start off the patterns shown below, for your child to continue.

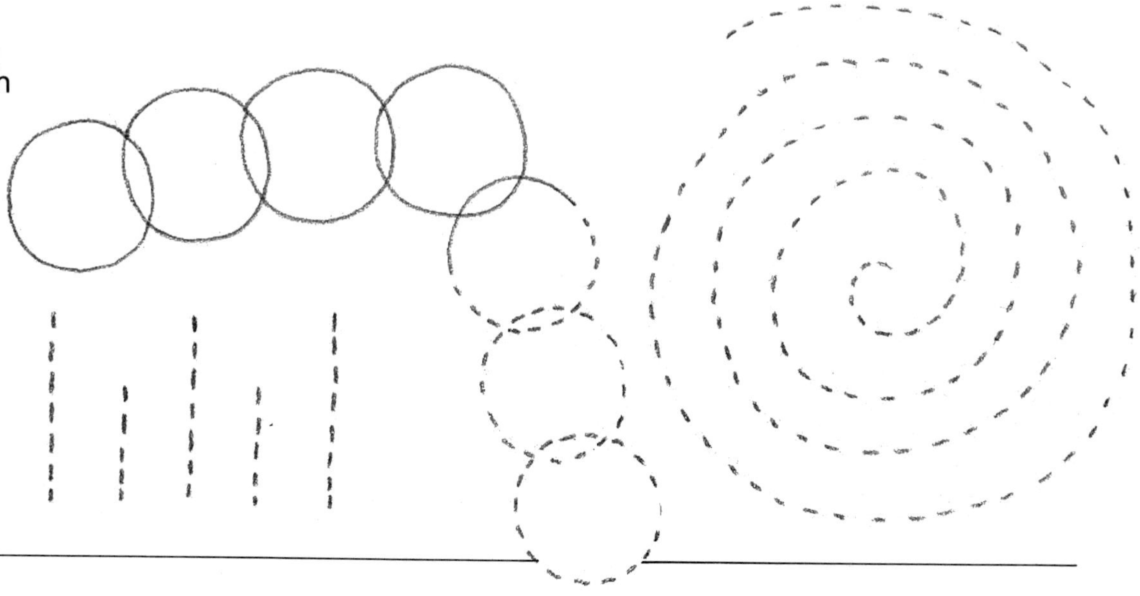

3 Make the patterns more fun by combining several together, or turn some of them into pictures after your child has traced the basic pattern.

4 Draw five pictures on one side of a piece of paper. On the opposite side, in a different order, draw five other pictures that are related to the first ones. Then ask your child to join them up into pairs with a pencil line.

Following the same idea, join words to pictures; or for older children, join identical words or words in rhyming pairs.

5 Draw some simple mazes which move across the page either from left to right, or from top to bottom. Or draw 'muddles' to be sorted out, such as three balloons with three muddled strings. Let your child find the right routes by drawing over them with a crayon.

Observing details

Place a few objects on the table and ask your child to look at them carefully, taking note of their relative positions. Then ask your child to close their eyes while you remove an object. Can they guess which object is missing? As your child gains experience more items can be added to make the game more difficult.

Working From Left to Right
Make the following games with strips of card about 5 cm by 20 cm (2 ins by 8 ins).

1 Find the pair: Draw a simple object on the left-hand side of the card and separate it off from the rest of the card with a coloured line. Then draw three or four other objects on the card—one of which is identical to the first object.

Encourage your child to work from left to right as they pick out the identical object.

2 Make up some cards as before, but this time use stick people performing different actions. Again, match one of the actions to the drawing on the far left of the card. Your child could imitate the actions of the stick people, too.

3 To make the game a bit harder, try drawing faces with different expressions, for example, smiling with eyes open, smiling with eyes shut, sad with eyes open, sad with eyes shut, tear in eyes and no tear.

4 Spot the difference: Make some other sets of cards showing rows of identical objects, except that one of them is different. Then try doing this with letters too.

Learning letters

1 Write letters using as many different tools as you can, such as steamy windows, in a tray of sand, or using a thick paintbrush on newspaper.

2 Try to make the shapes of letters with your hands—perhaps by using shadows on a sunny wall.

3 Look for letters on food packets, newspapers and magazines. Make up cards for each letter showing all the different ways they can appear in print.

4 Make up some other cards with two or three versions of two or three letters all mixed up. Ask your child to find the versions of one letter.

Or, cut out some words which each contain one particular letter (such as 'a'). Then ask your child to find and circle that letter in each word.

5 Cut out letters from black paper and trace them onto a sheet of white paper. Let your child match the silhouette to the outline.

6 Play 'Find the pair' and 'Spot the difference' as described on the previous pages, but this time using letters instead of objects.

Letter games

1 Make some sets of letter cards to play snap, pairs, lotto and dominoes (see pages 99-102 for details of games).

2 Make a simple board game with some squares coloured in—as shown in the illustration. Put a stack of letter cards face down in the middle of the board. Take turns to throw a dice and move round the board. When a player lands on a coloured square he or she has to pick up a letter card and say the name of the letter. If the answer is right the player wins another throw of the dice.

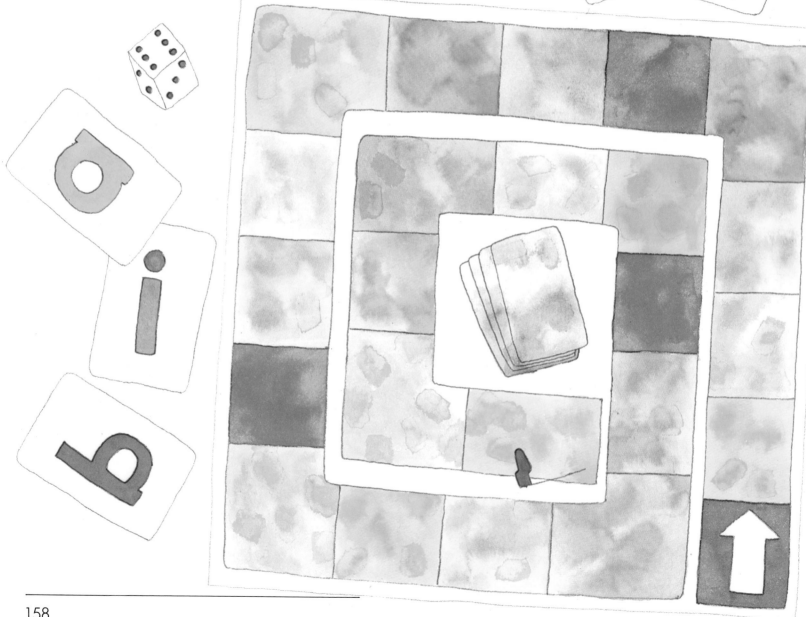

Learning words

Making and Using Word Cards

As you read simple books with your child, print the words they are learning in large letters onto pieces of card. Always be certain that the words you use have first been read within the context of a sentence.

1 Let your child search for simple words ('and', 'the', 'my') in his or her books, then match the word to the appropriate word card.

2 Make cards showing the names of members of your family. Use them as place-names on chairs or at the table.

3 Label objects in the house. Extend this idea to introducing short phrases as well, such as 'Daddy's chair' and 'Mary's cup'.

4 Posters made out of pictures cut from magazines can also be labelled.

Action Cards

Once your child is beginning to feel confident with reading words, there are many ways to encourage their understanding of words. Here are a few suggestions:

1 Draw stick people on cards with each one performing a different action. Write the word for the action on the appropriate card. Hold up the cards one at a time for your child to read the word and imitate the action.

2 Write out simple instruction cards for different actions. Place the cards in a line across the room. Your child has to move from one card to the next, reading and then carrying out the instructions.

3 Hide an object and give your child a card which tells them where to find it. For example, 'look under the table'. As their skill improves, extend the hunt by hiding the cards around the house, one card giving the clue to the next and the final one leading to the 'treasure'.

Word games

Sorting
There are many ways to sort words. For example, word cards can be posted into boxes according to their initial letters, or into trays according to their subject matter.

Card Games
Use the word cards, either by themselves or with matching picture cards, to play snap, pairs, lotto and dominoes (see pages 99-102 for details about the games).

Hidden Pictures
Fold a piece of card firmly in half. Write a word that your child has learnt on the outside and stick a picture to illustrate the word on the inside. If your child has difficulty reading the word, they can use the picture as a clue.

Adjectives
Cut out pictures from magazines and birthday cards (or draw them) to illustrate adjectives. Stick them on cards and write the adjective and noun underneath, for example, 'thin dog', 'fat dog', and so on.

Fishing
Slip a paper clip onto each of your word cards and put them into a large cardboard box. Make a fishing line using a stick, and some string with a magnet tied to the end of it. Take turns to fish out a card and read it out. Any that can't be read are thrown back into the 'pool' for another go (but make certain to read out the word first so that the next time it is caught it may be remembered).

Opposites
Make some more cards that will illustrate opposites, such as 'up' and 'down', 'in' and 'out', 'on' and 'off'.

Plurals
Take a piece of card and fold a third of it back. Write down the singular of any noun that forms its plural with an 's' (dog, cat, ball, bird, hat) on the front of the card on the left-hand side. Write the 's' on the far side of the folded piece so that when it is folded on top of the card the word becomes a plural. Illustrate the word and the 's' with matching pictures.